VALENTINE'S DAY

COLORING BOOK FOR TODDLERS

THIS BOOK BELONGS TO:

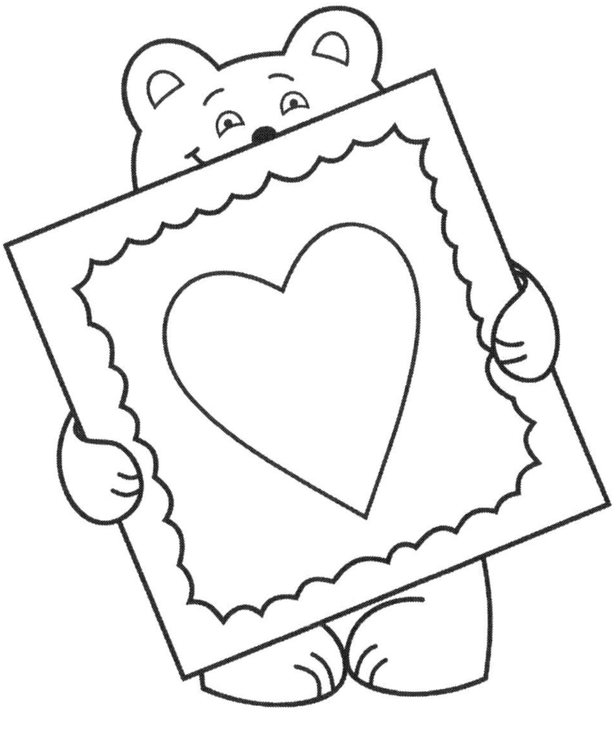

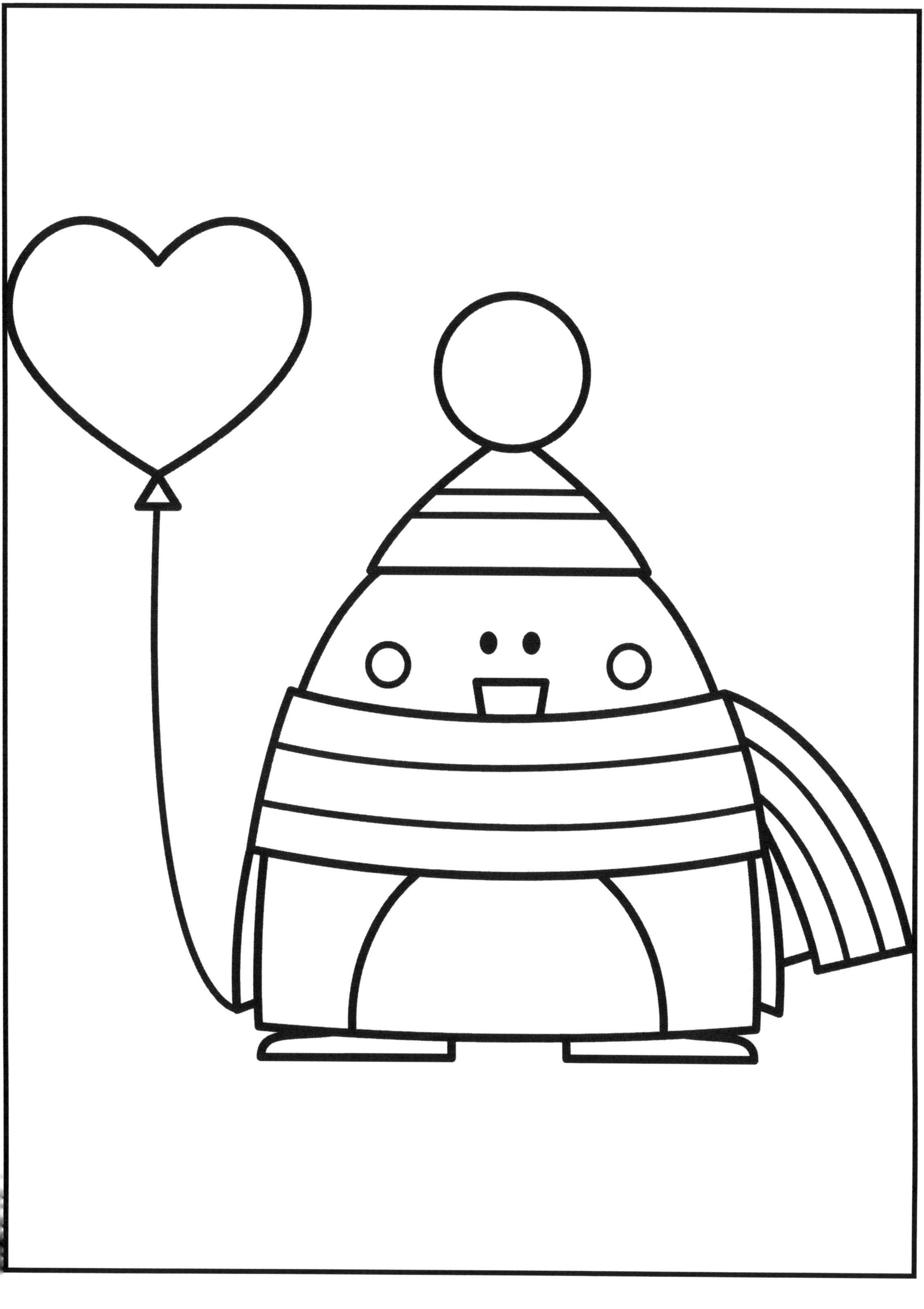

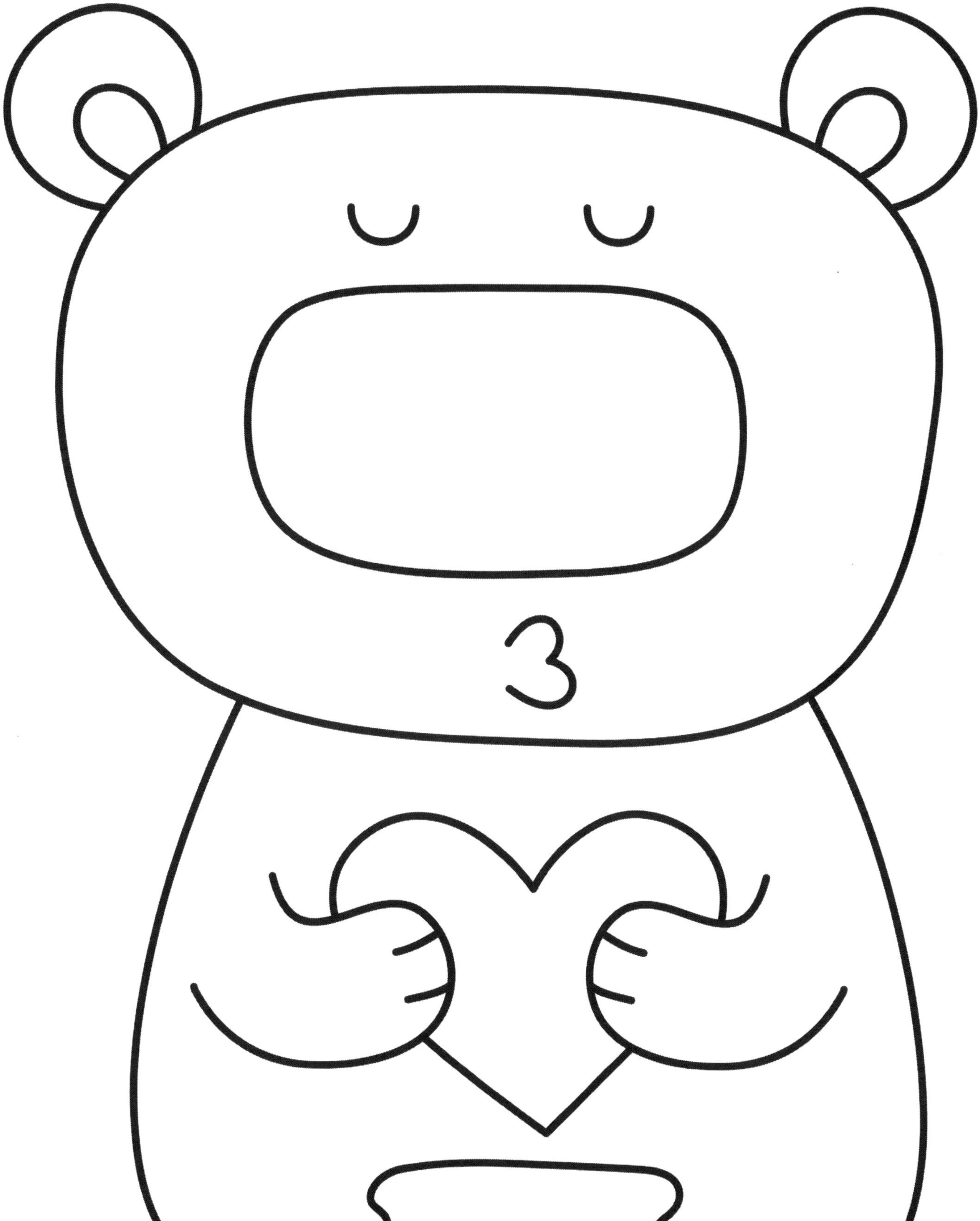

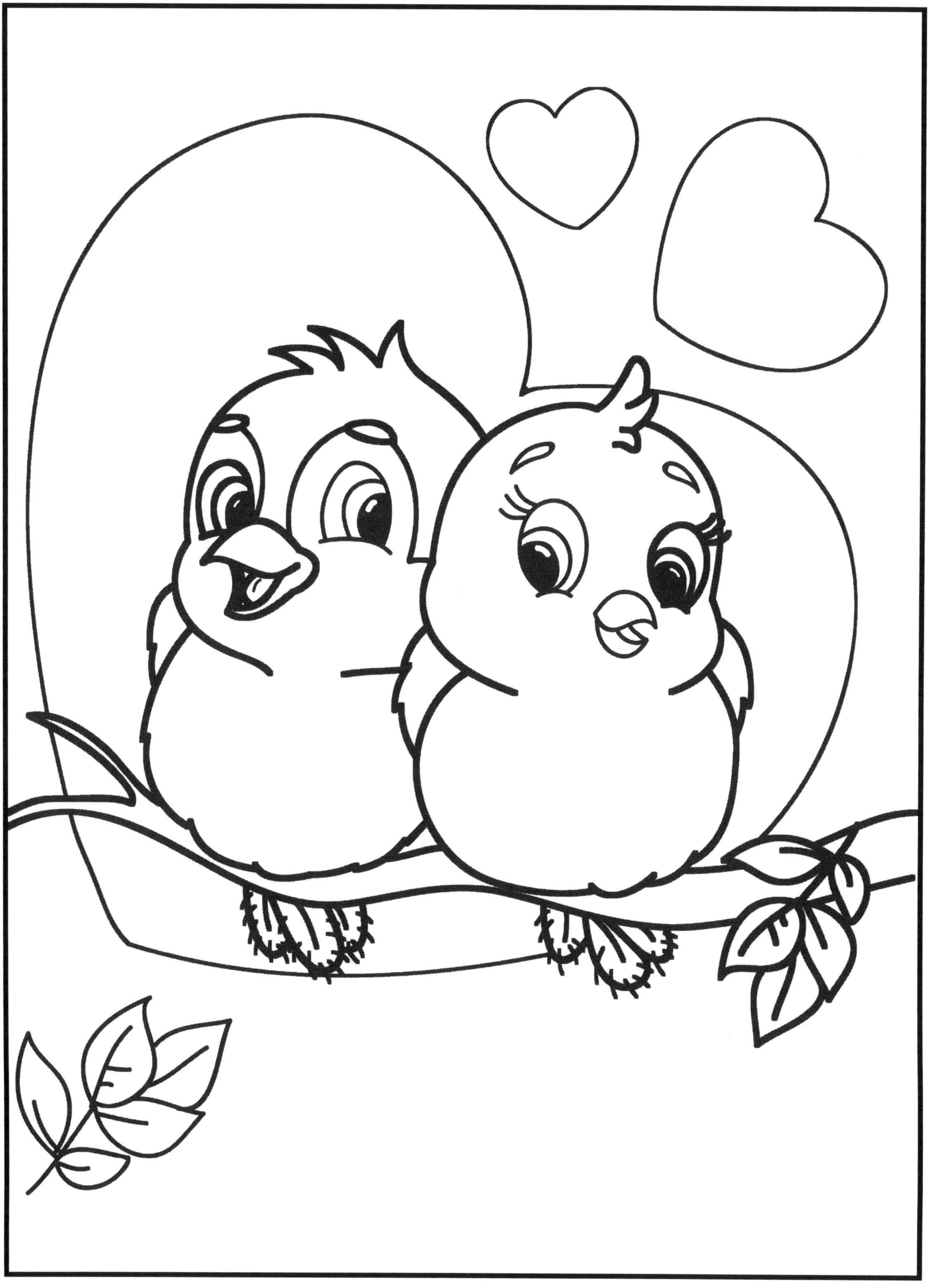

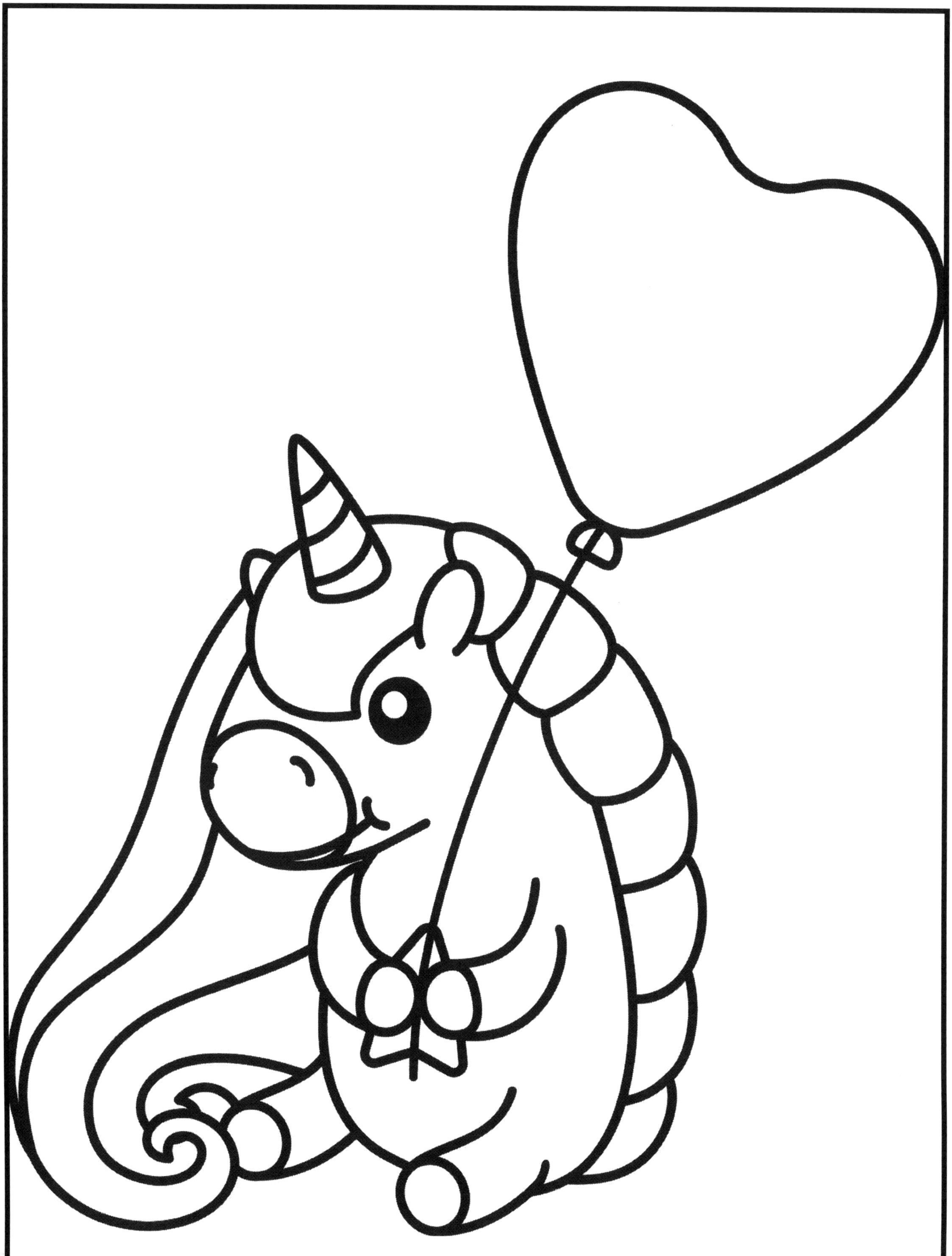

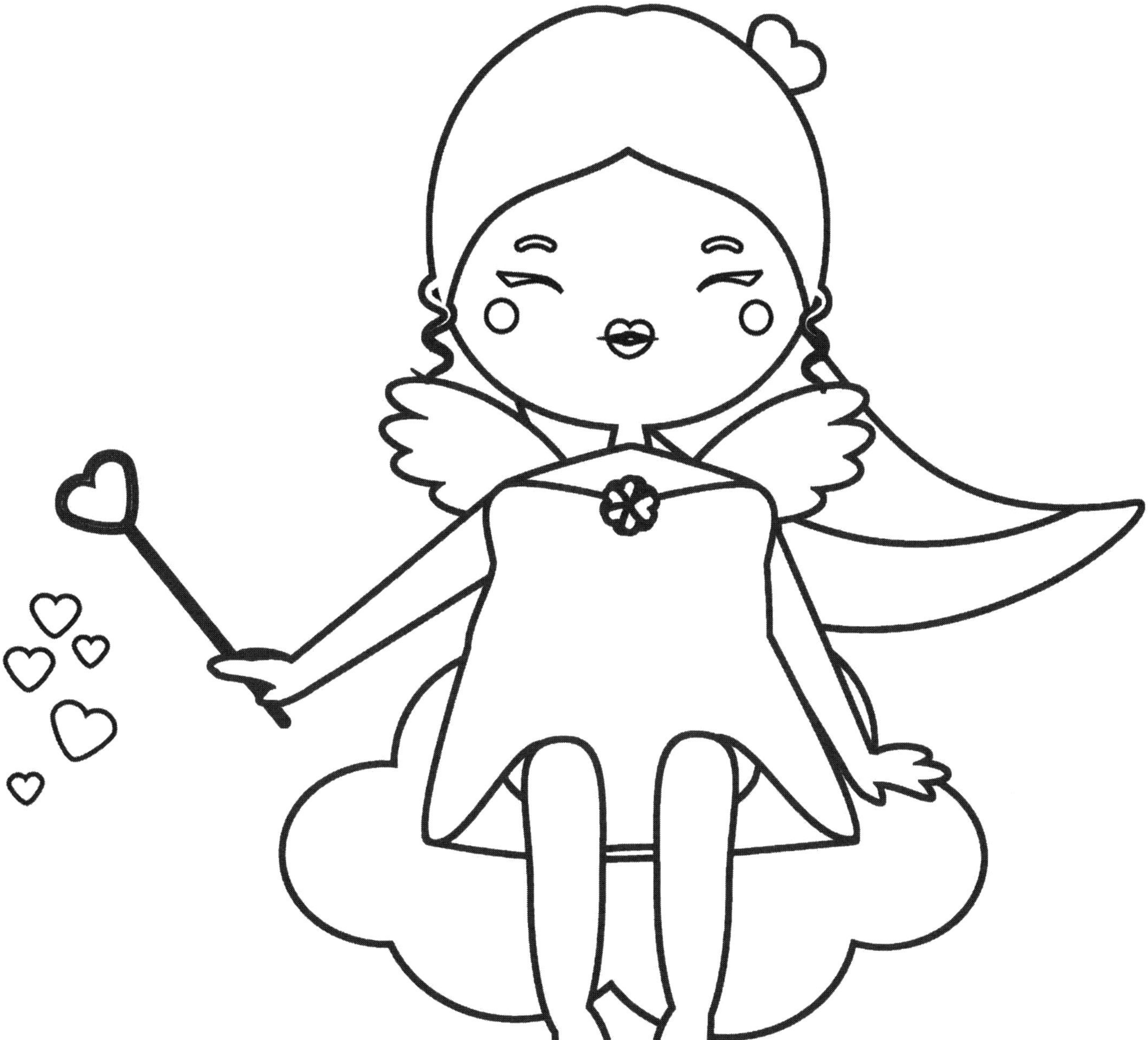

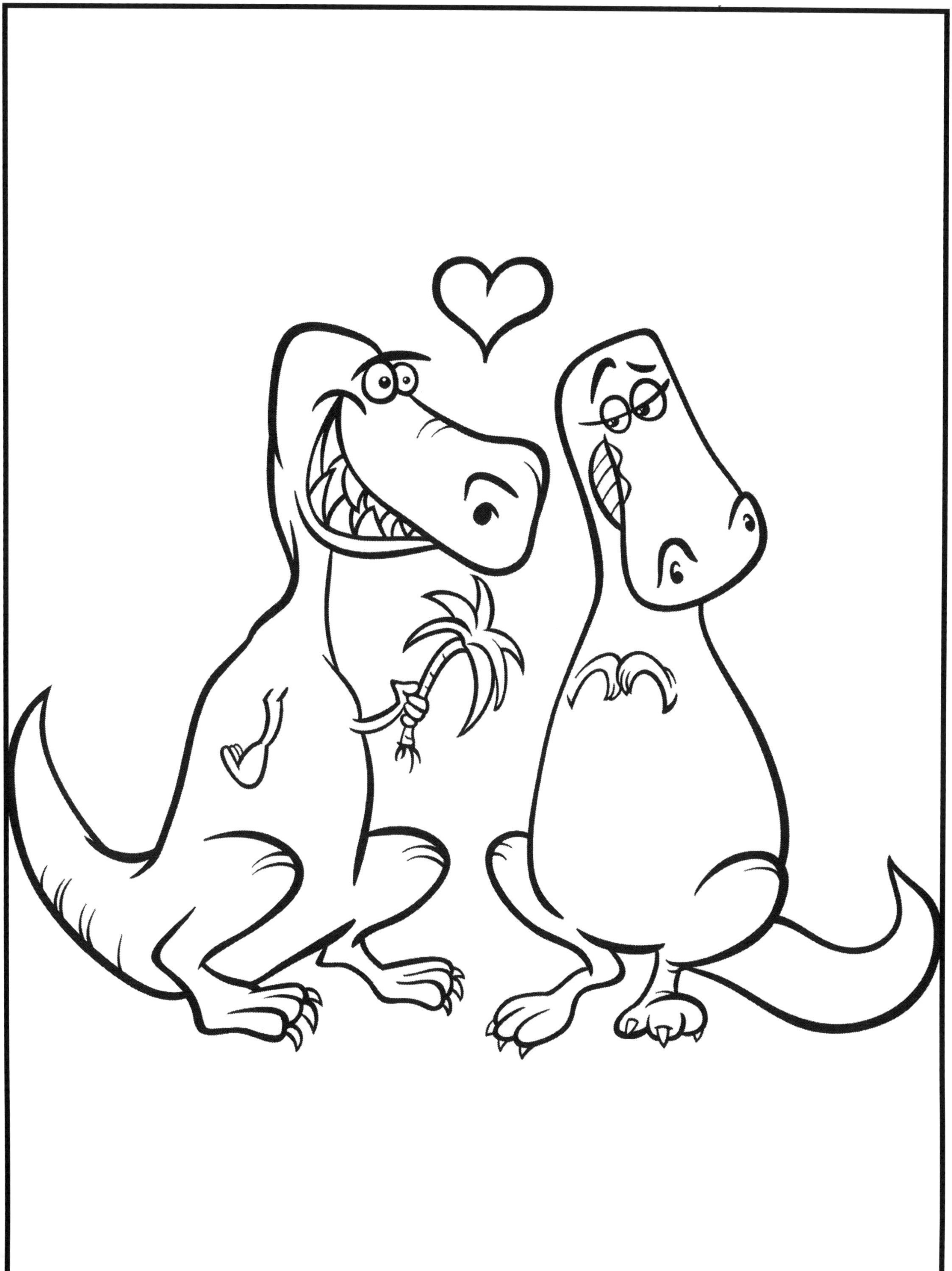

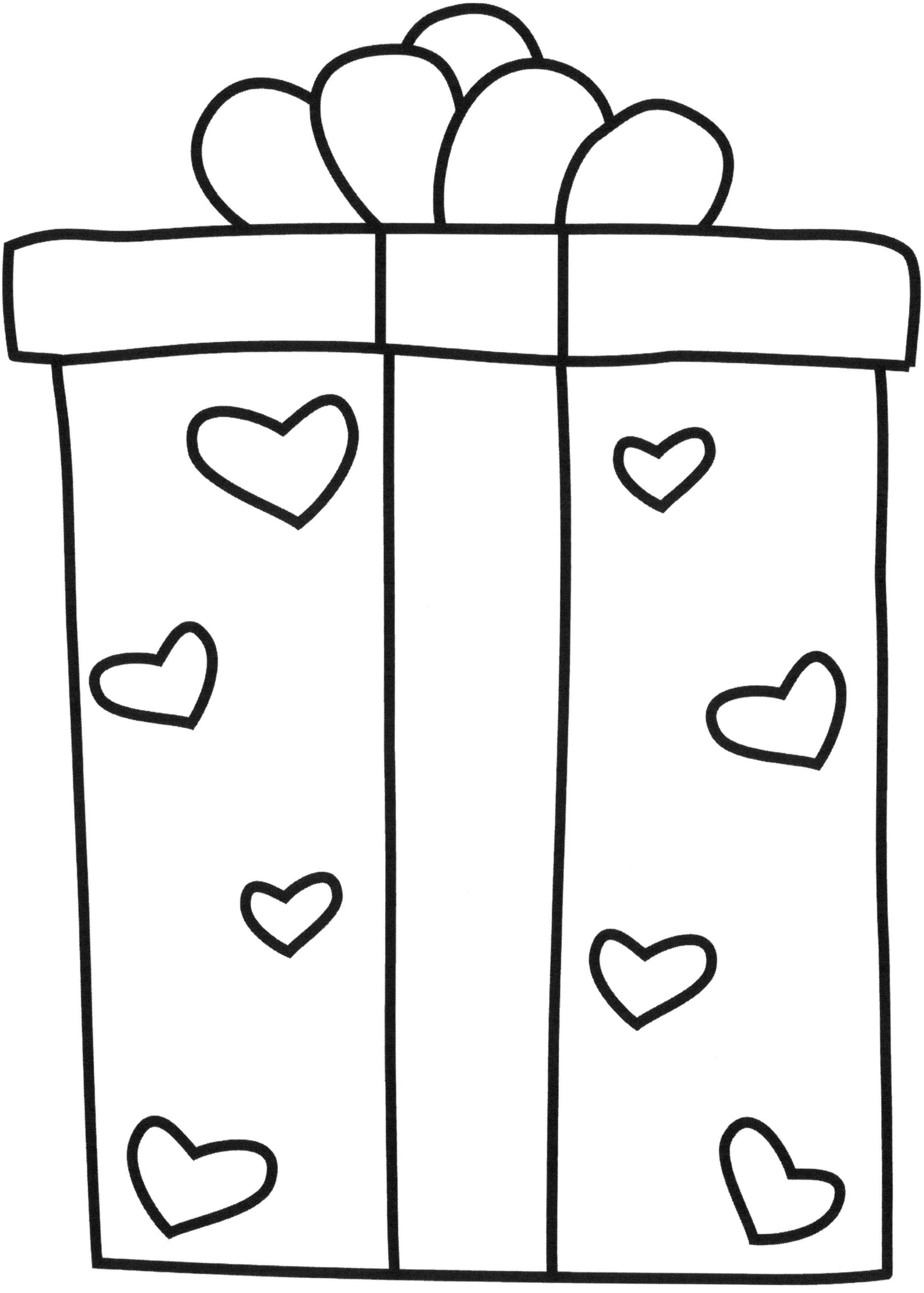

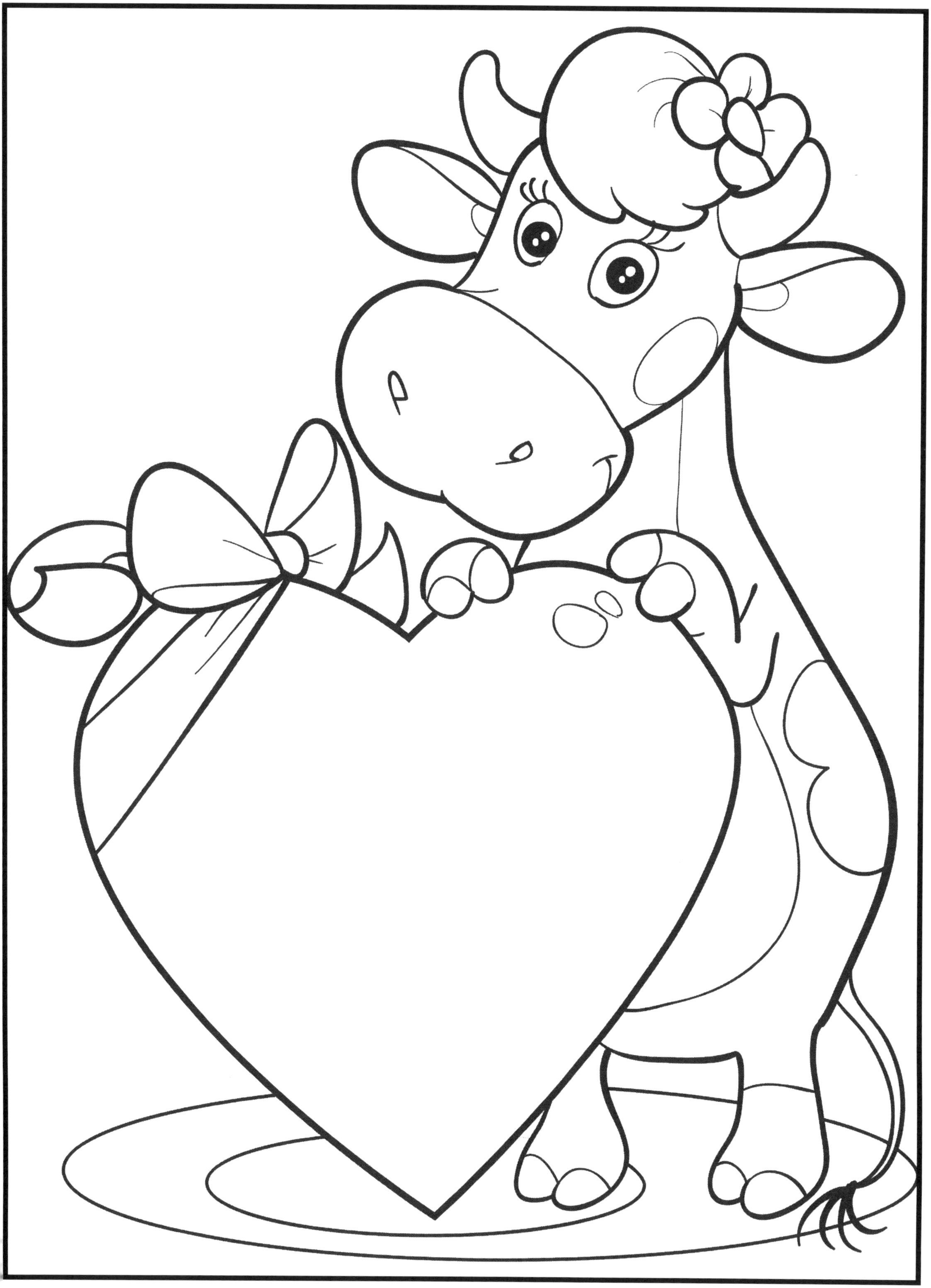

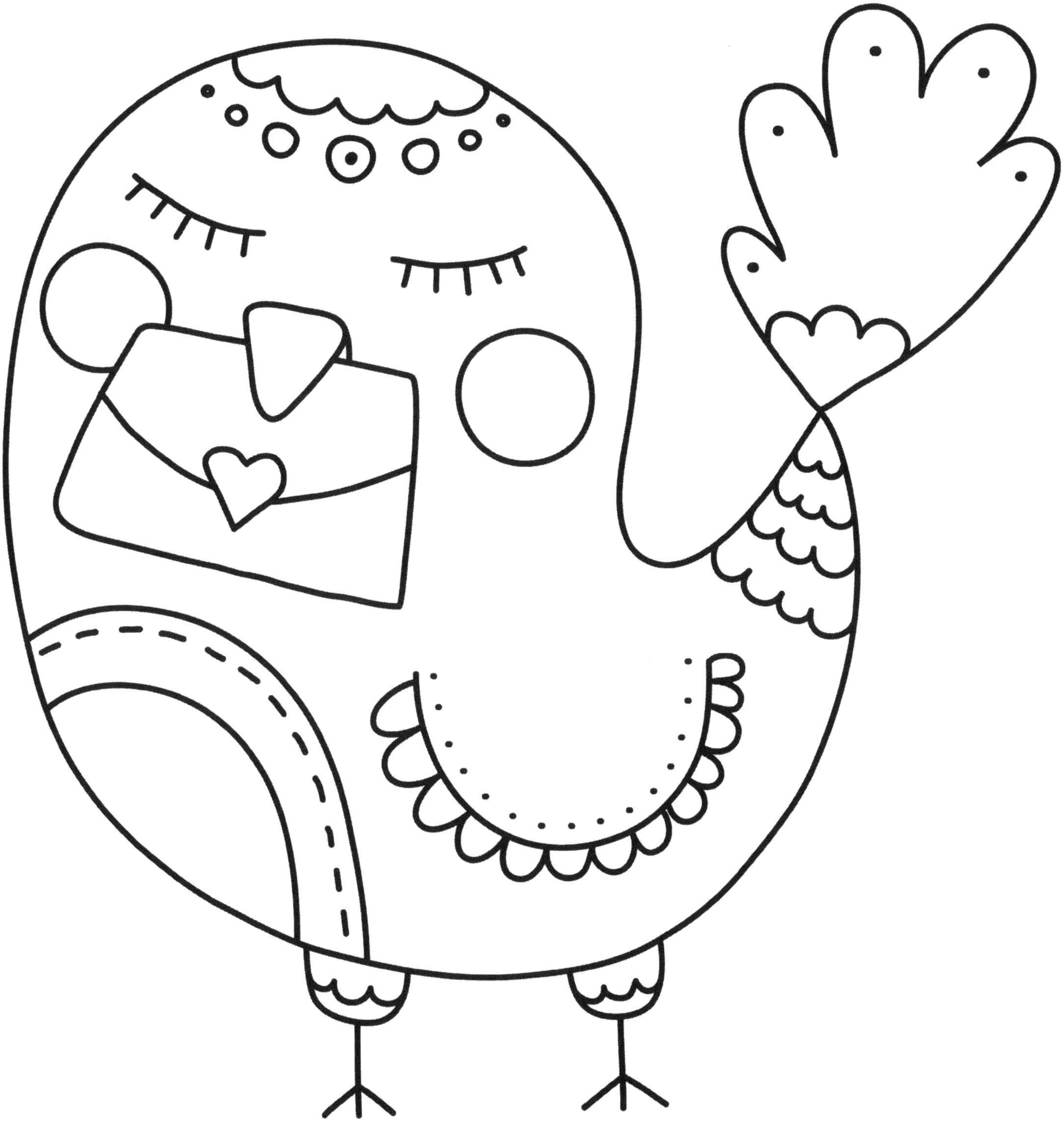

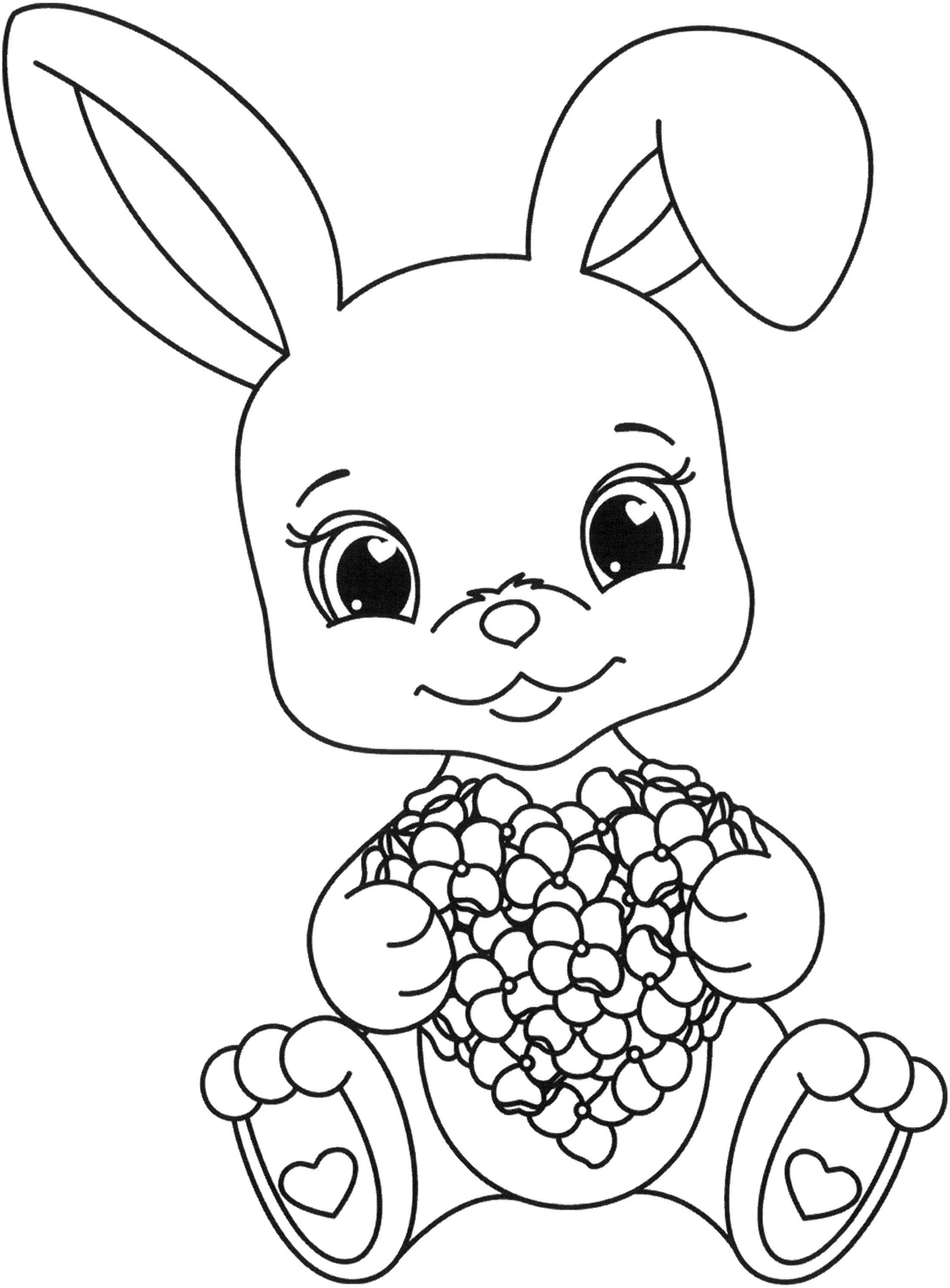

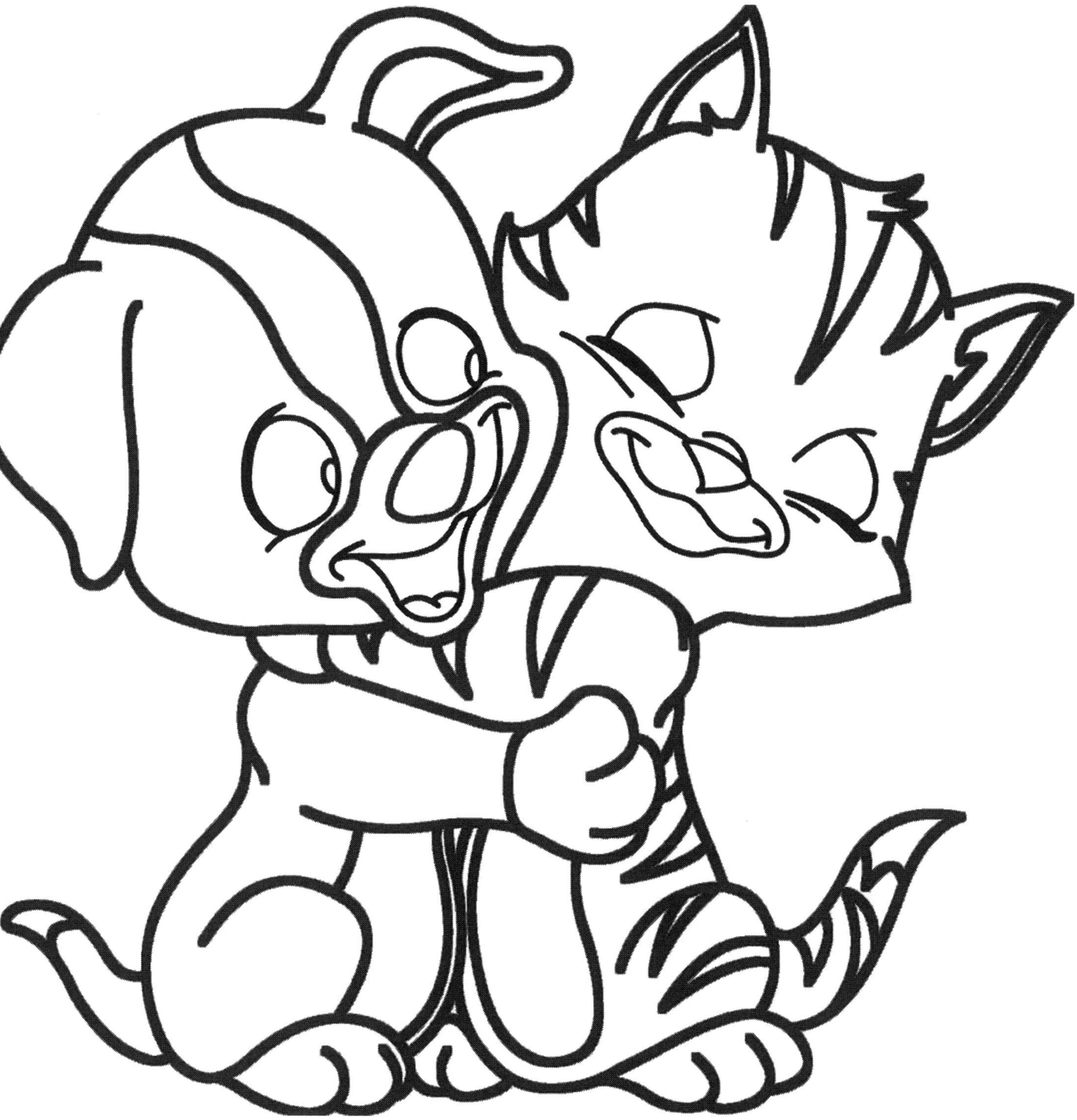

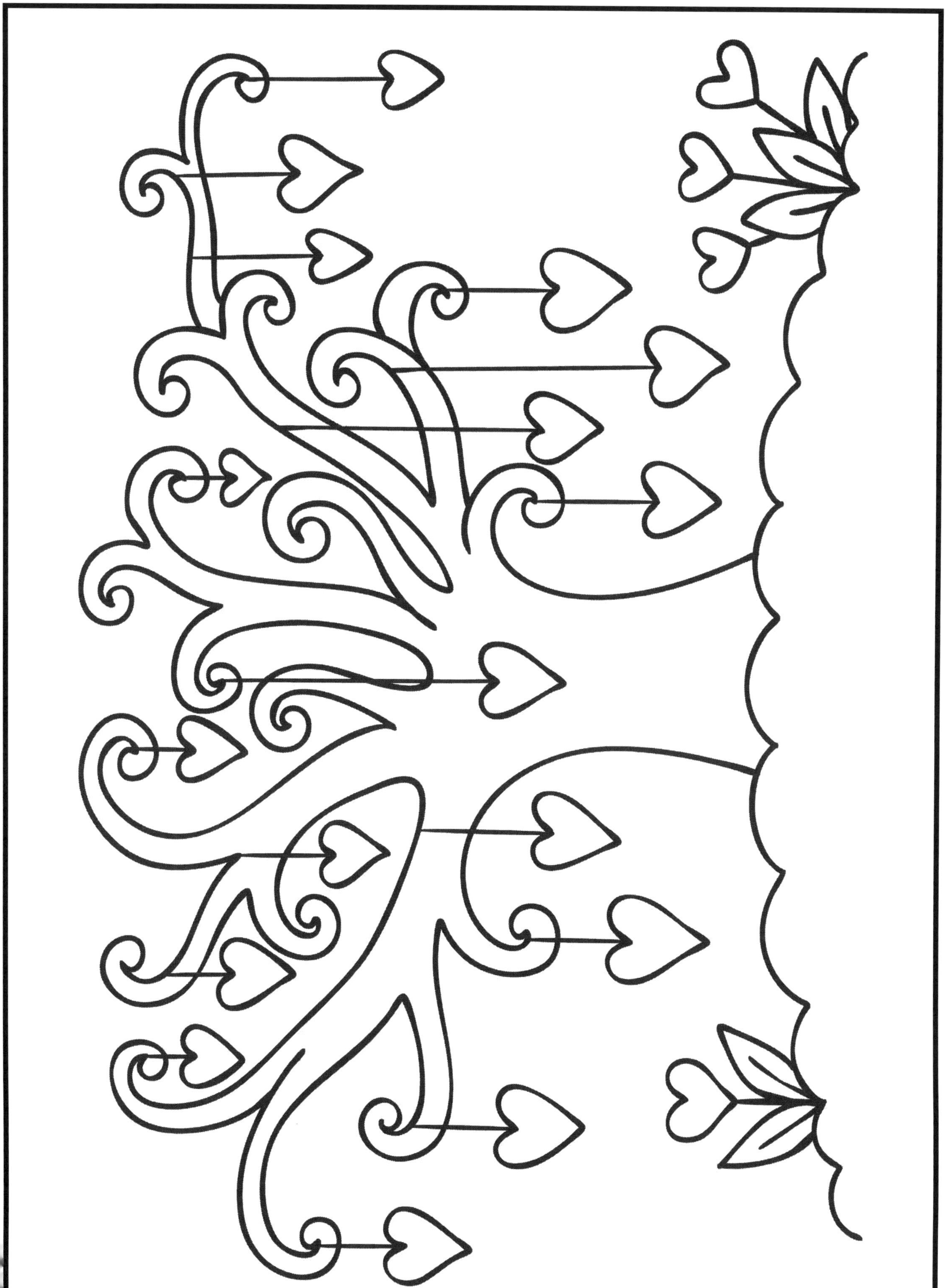

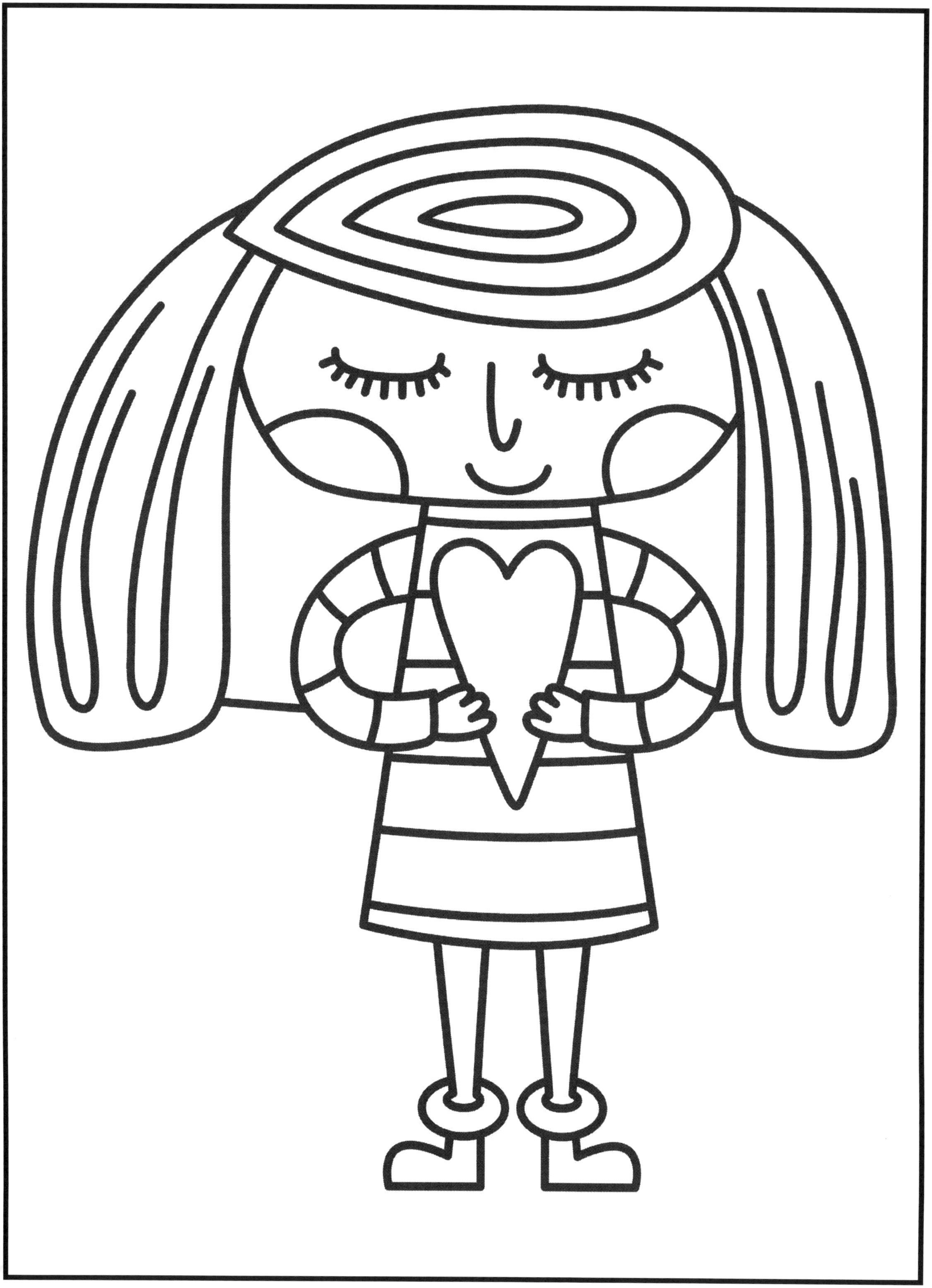

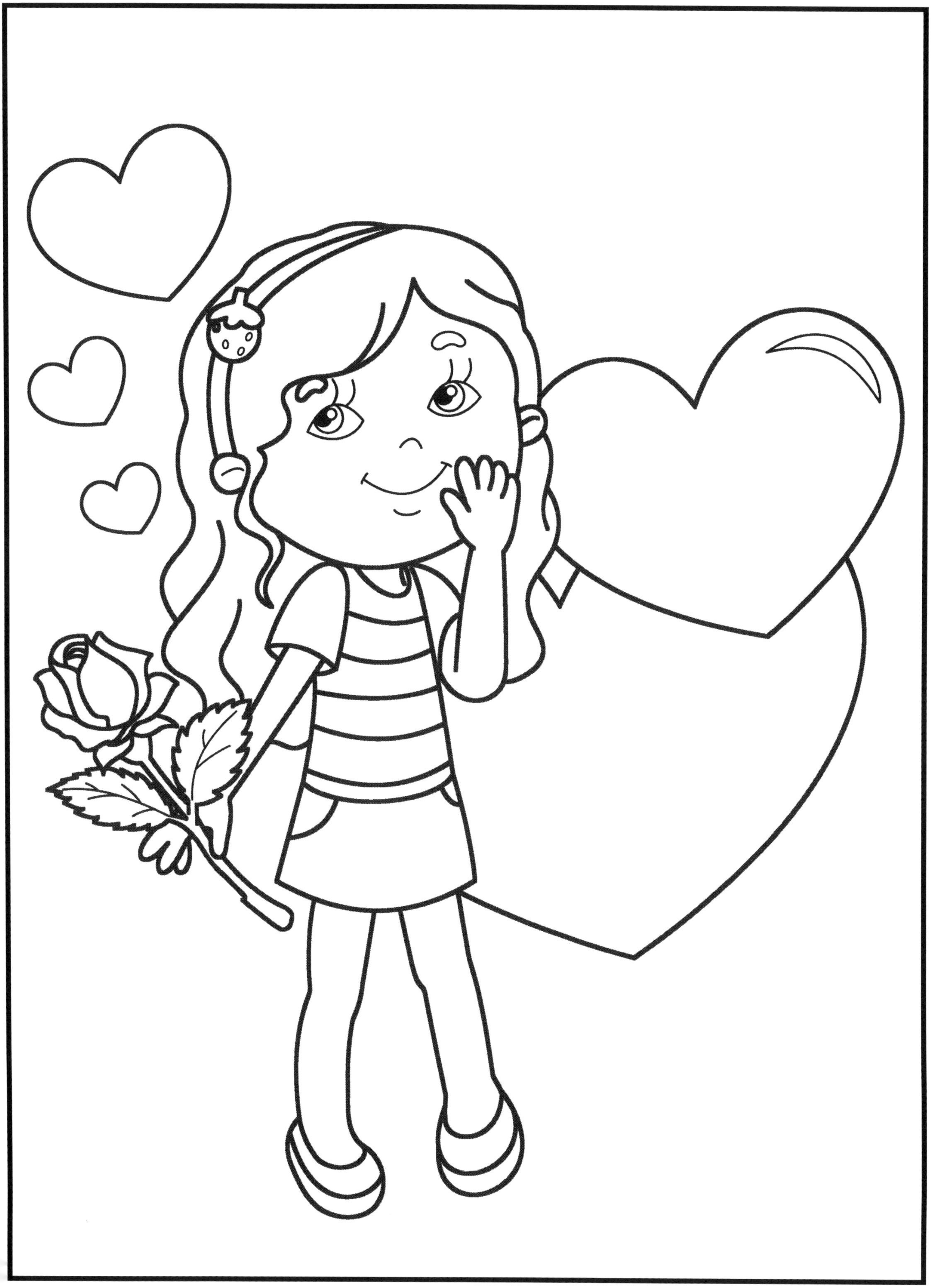

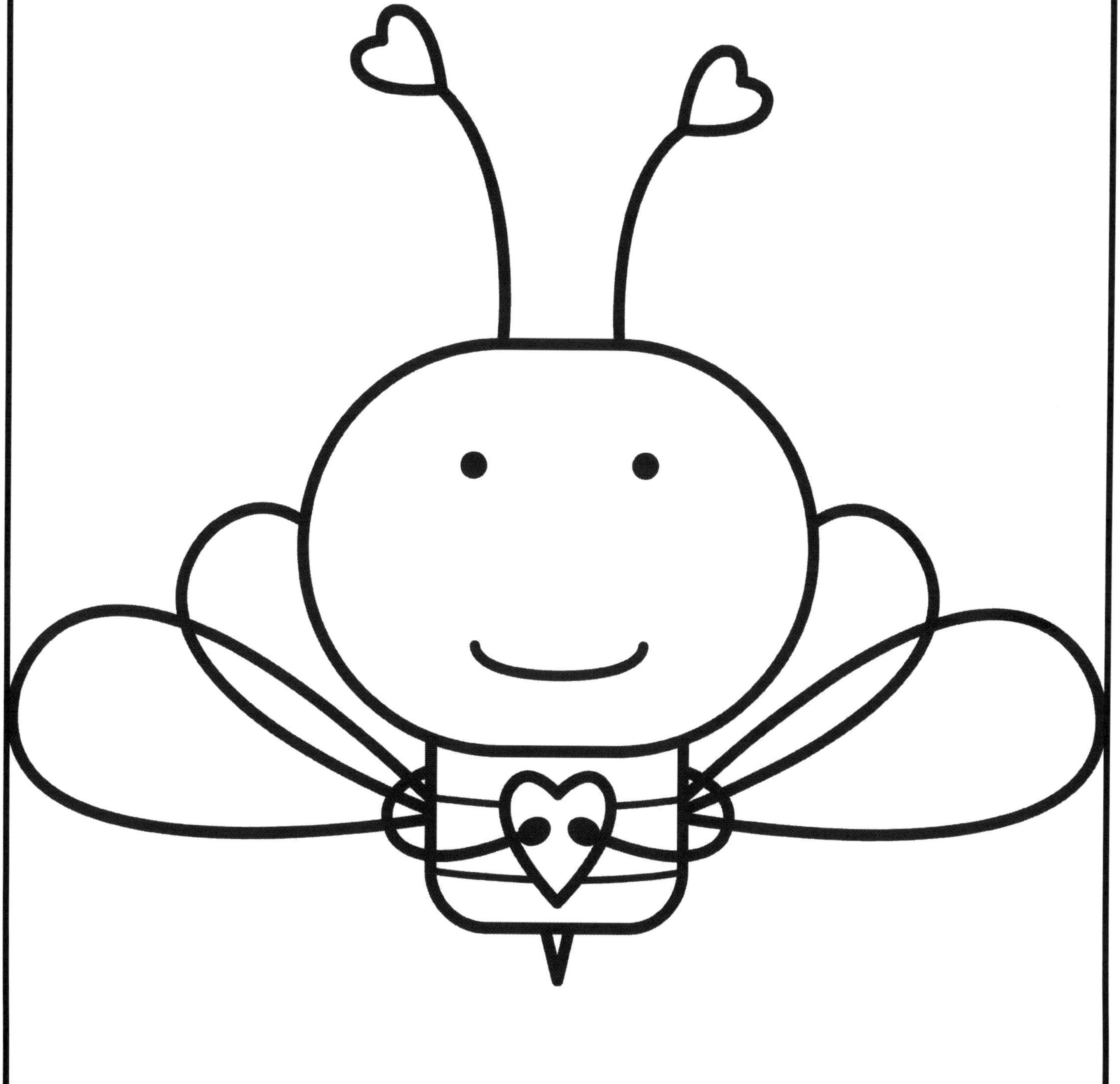

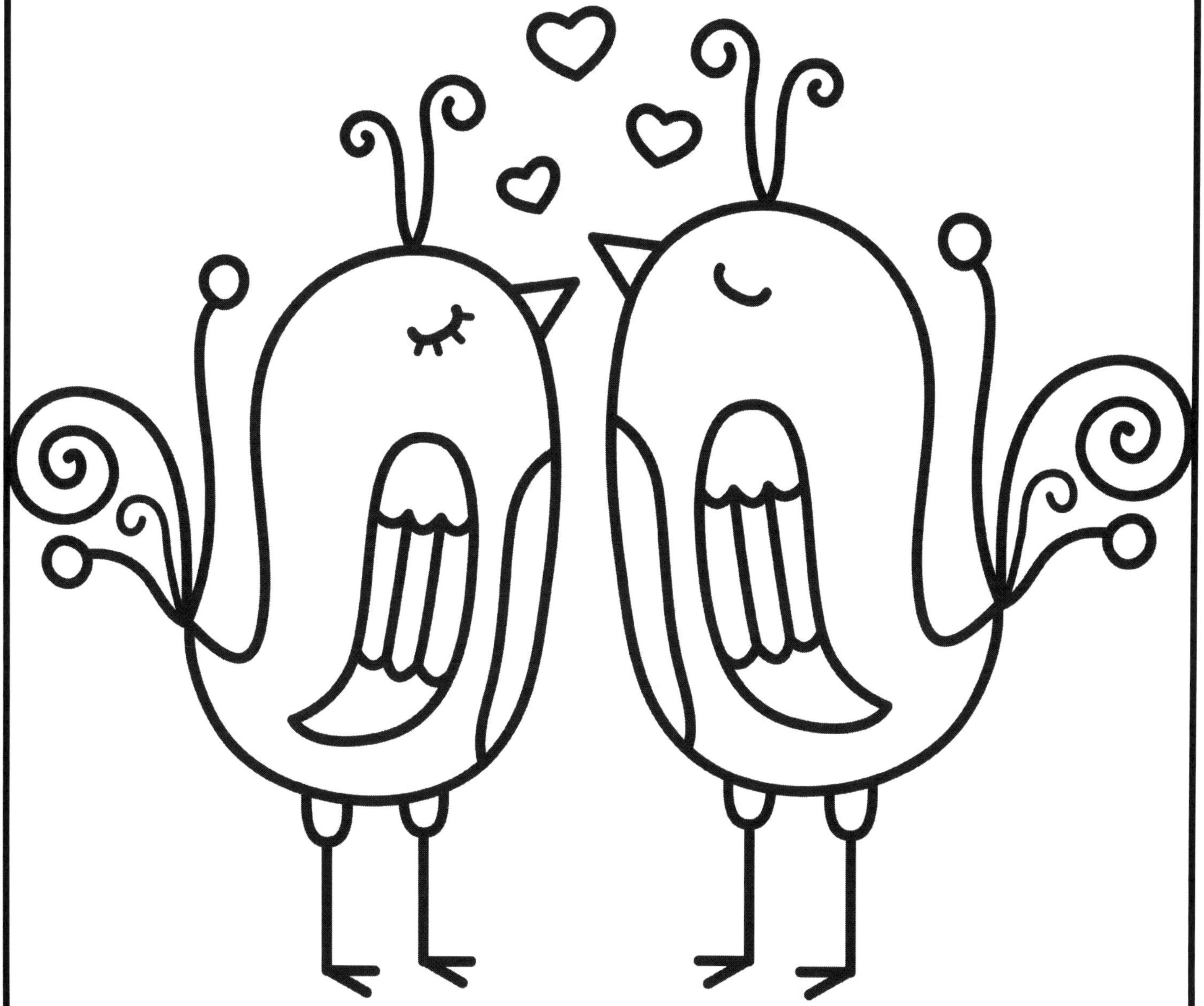

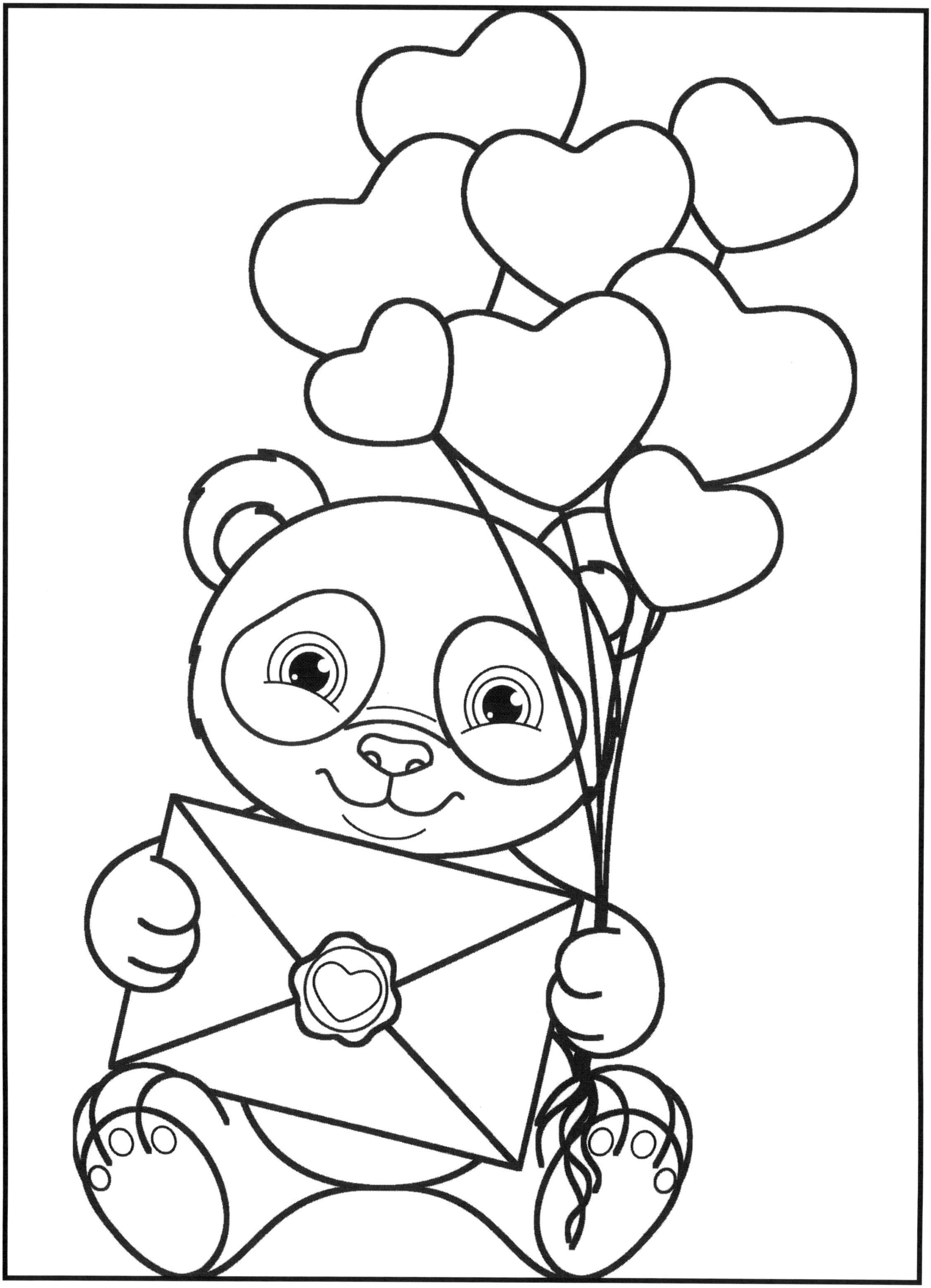

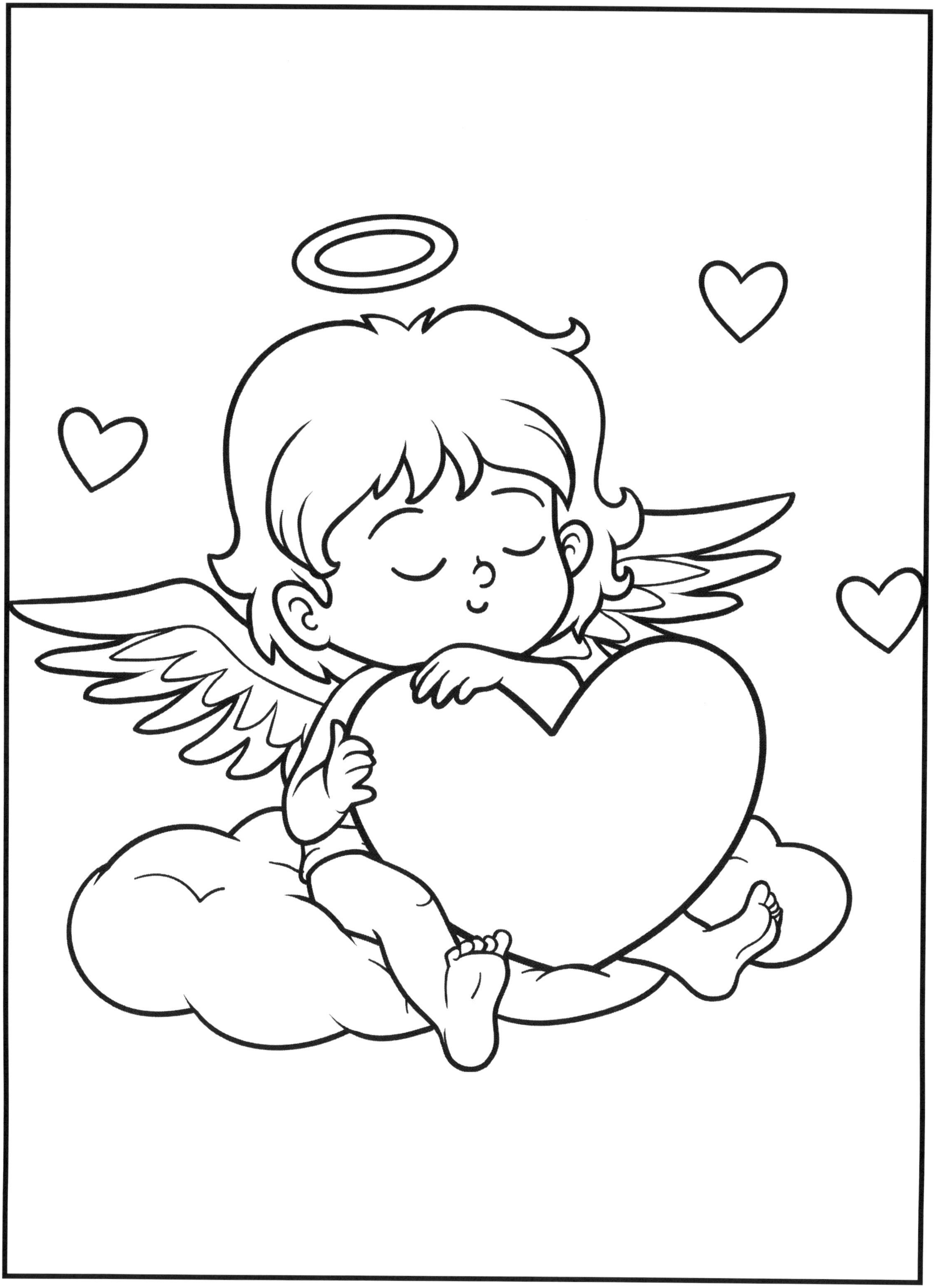

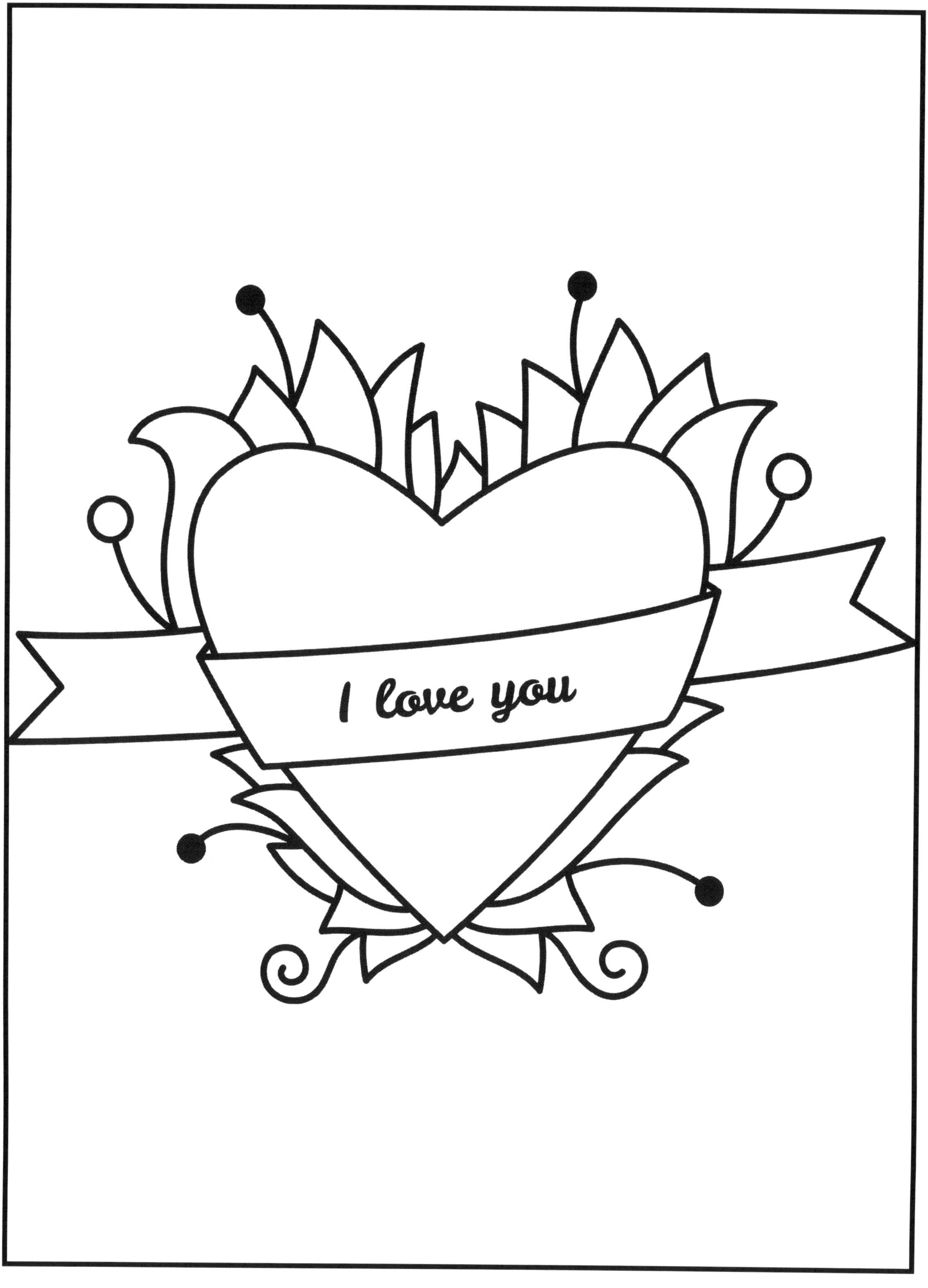
I love you

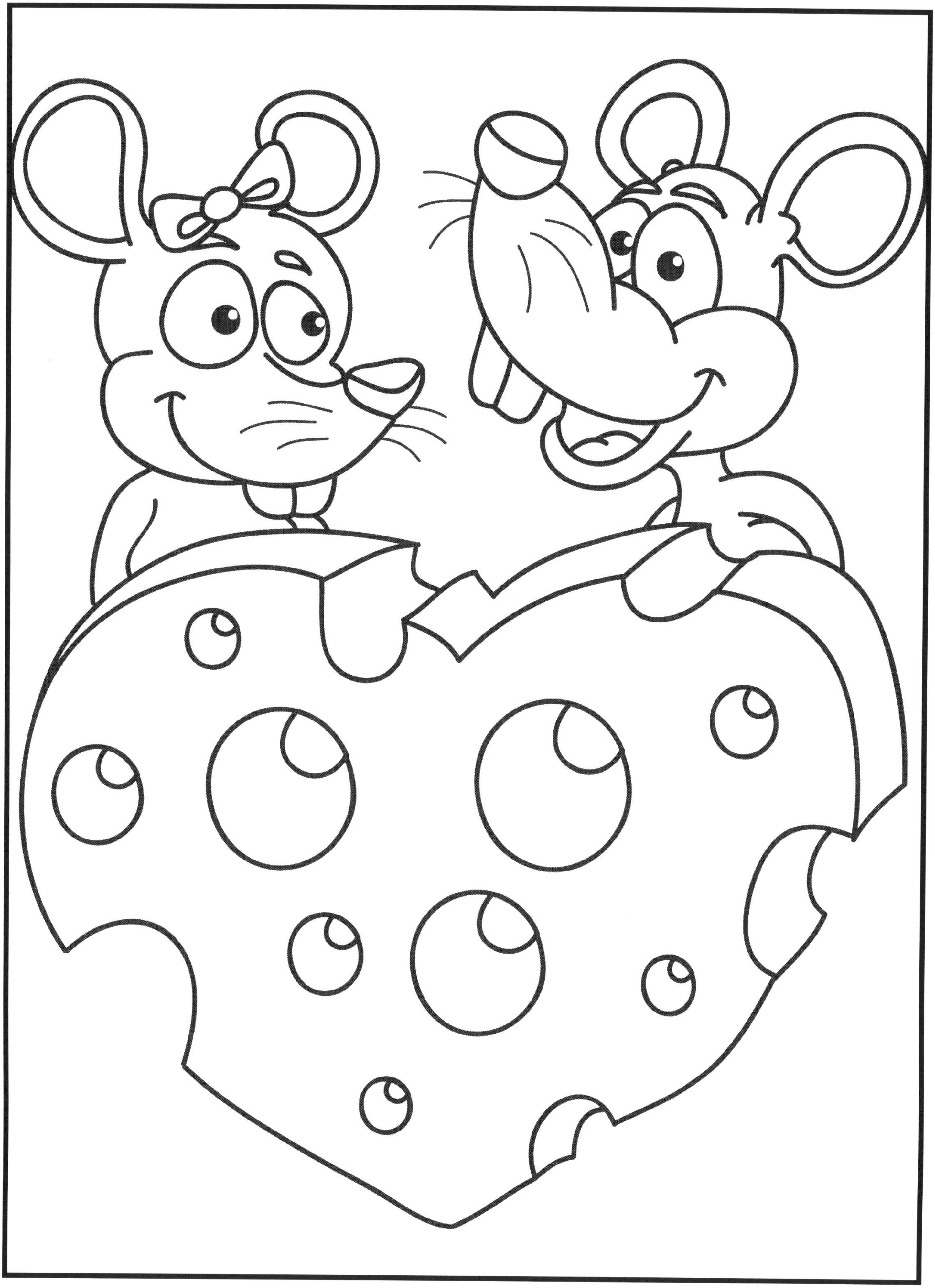

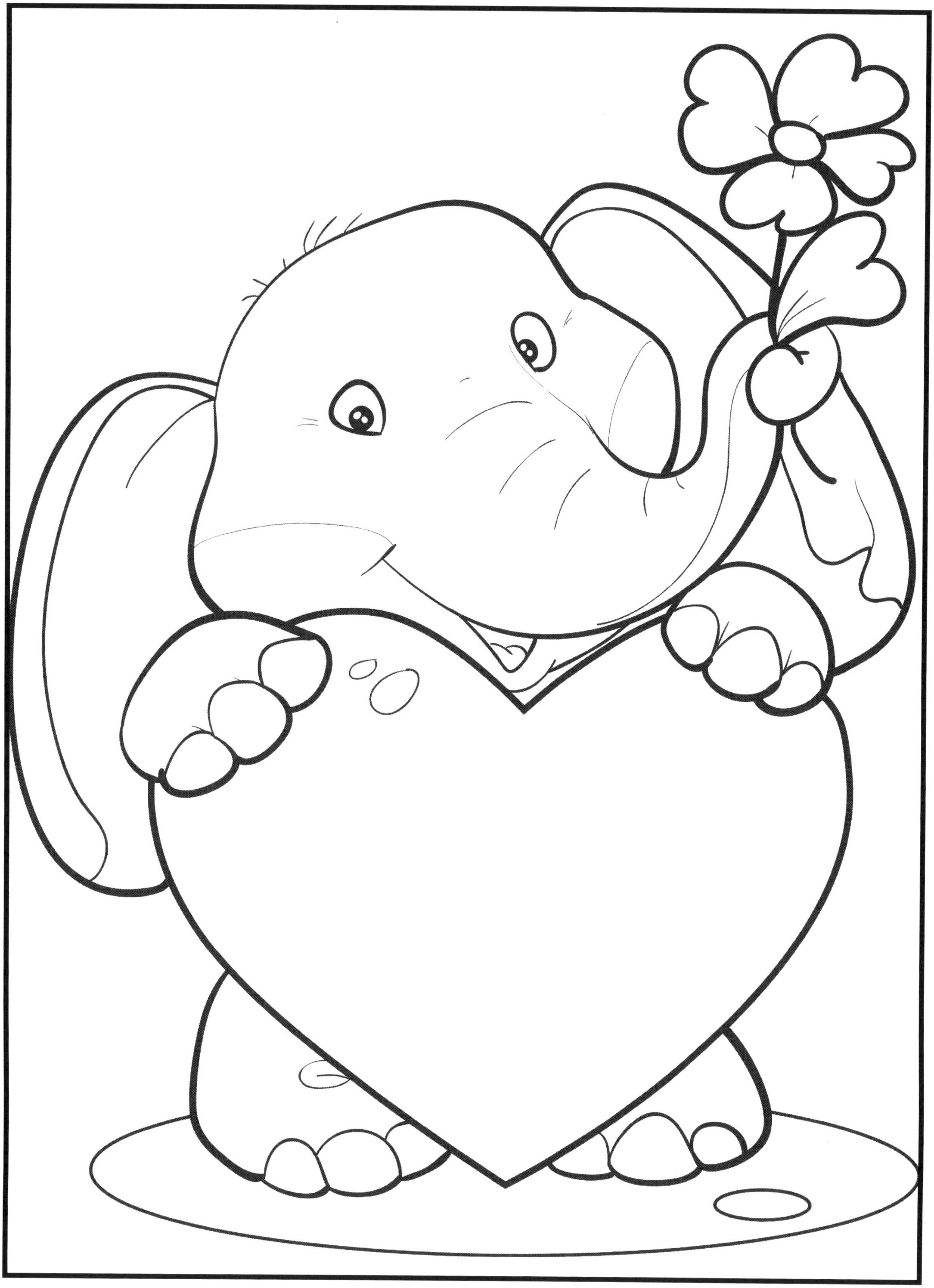

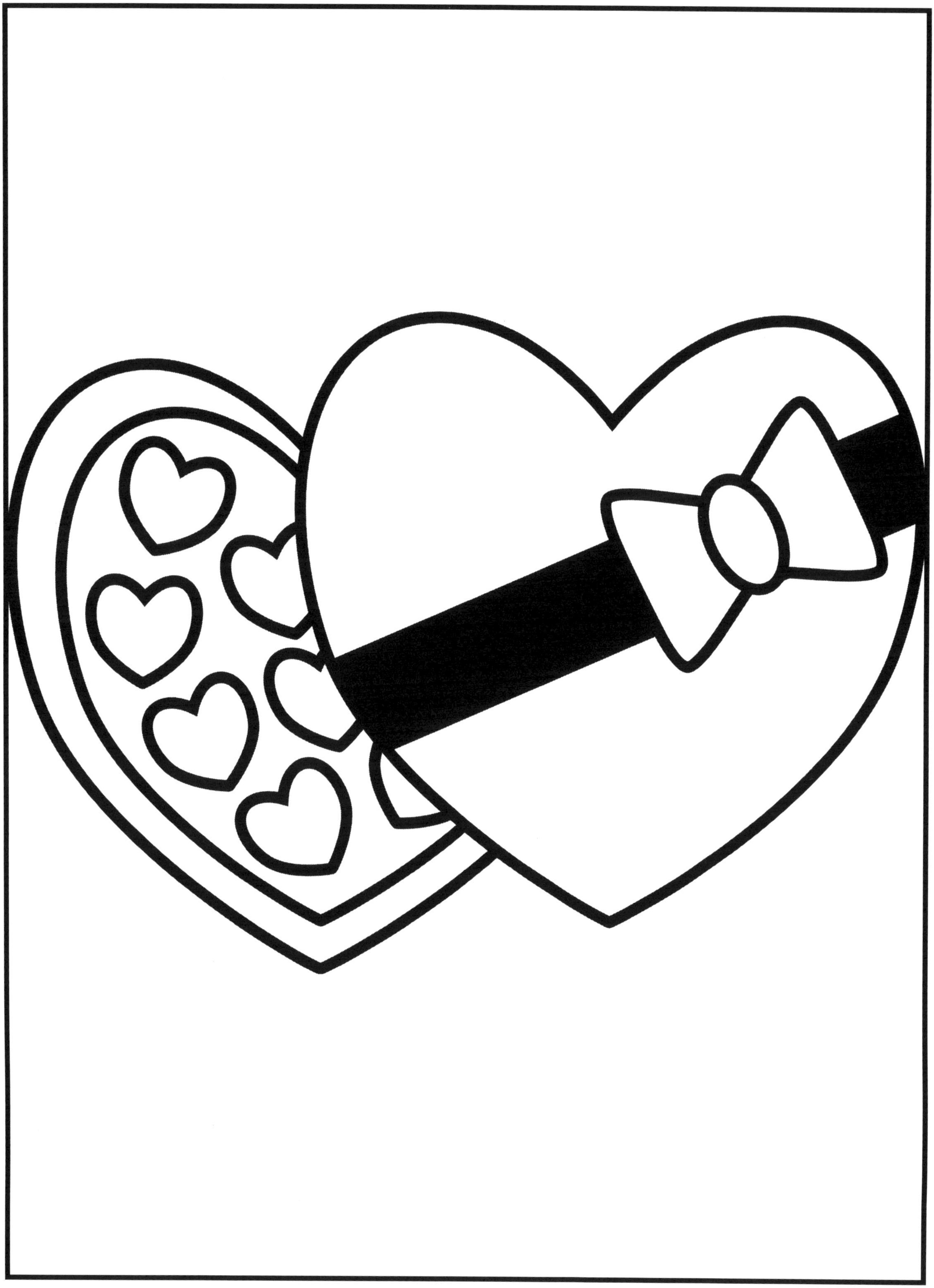

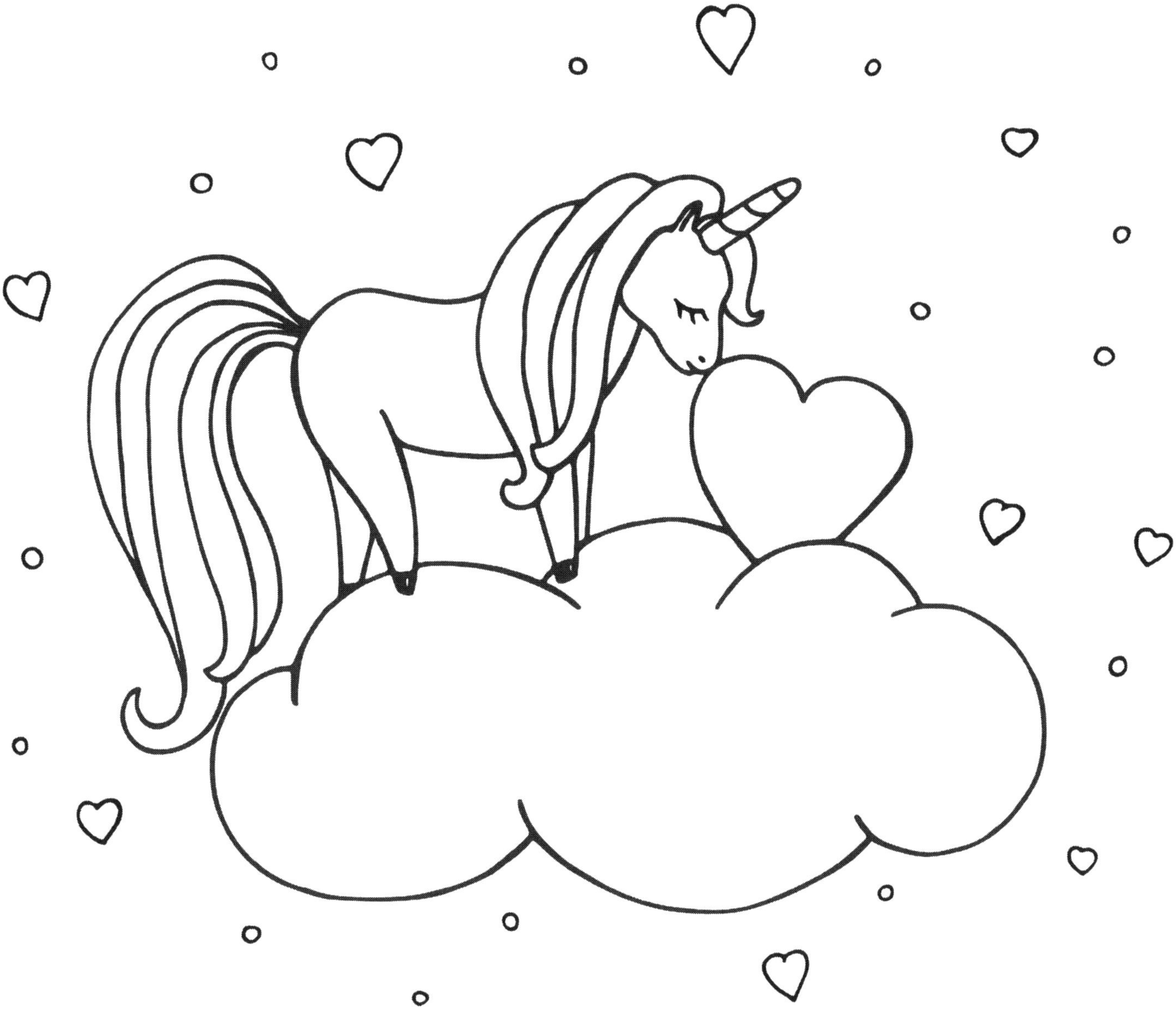

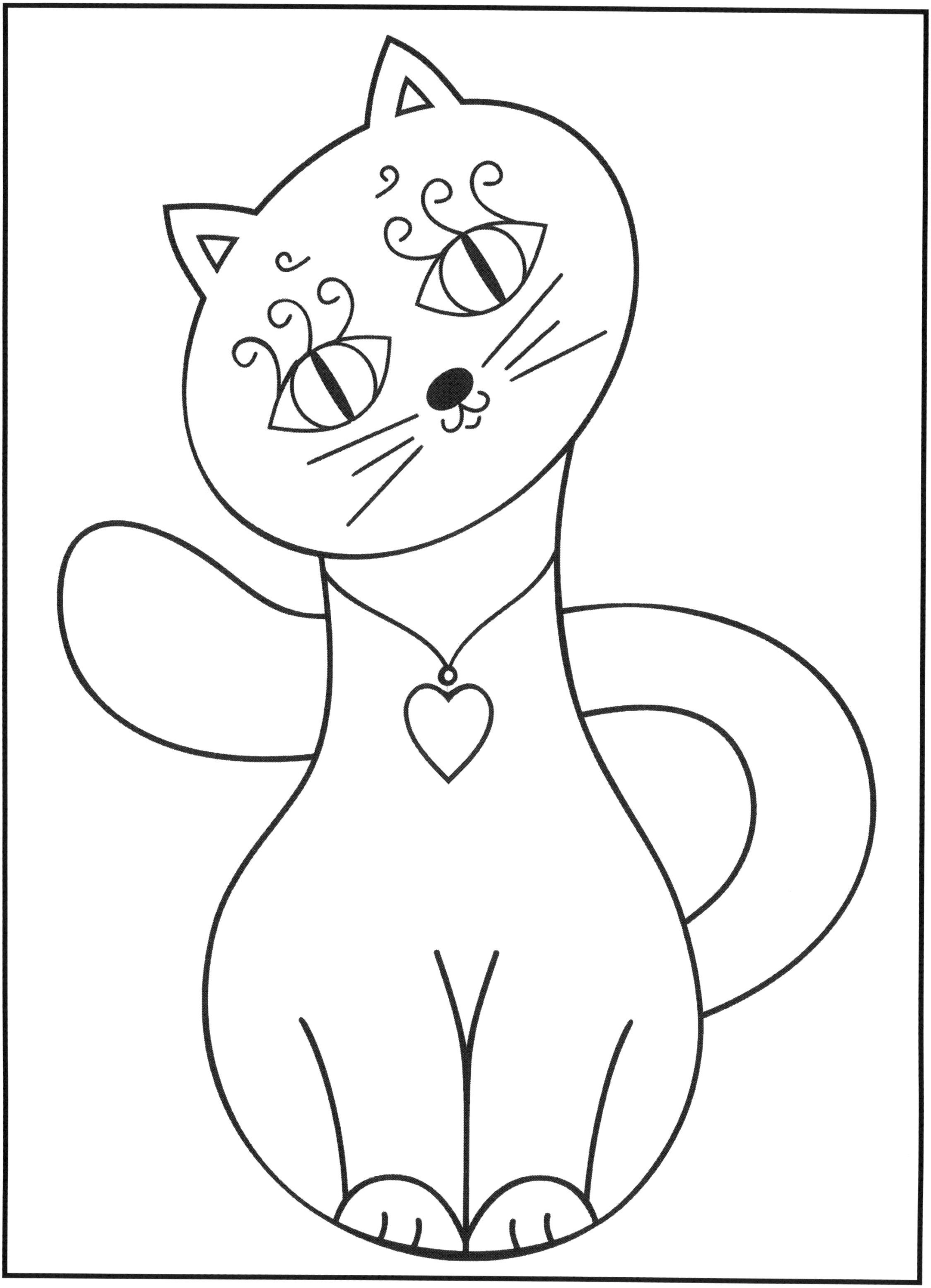

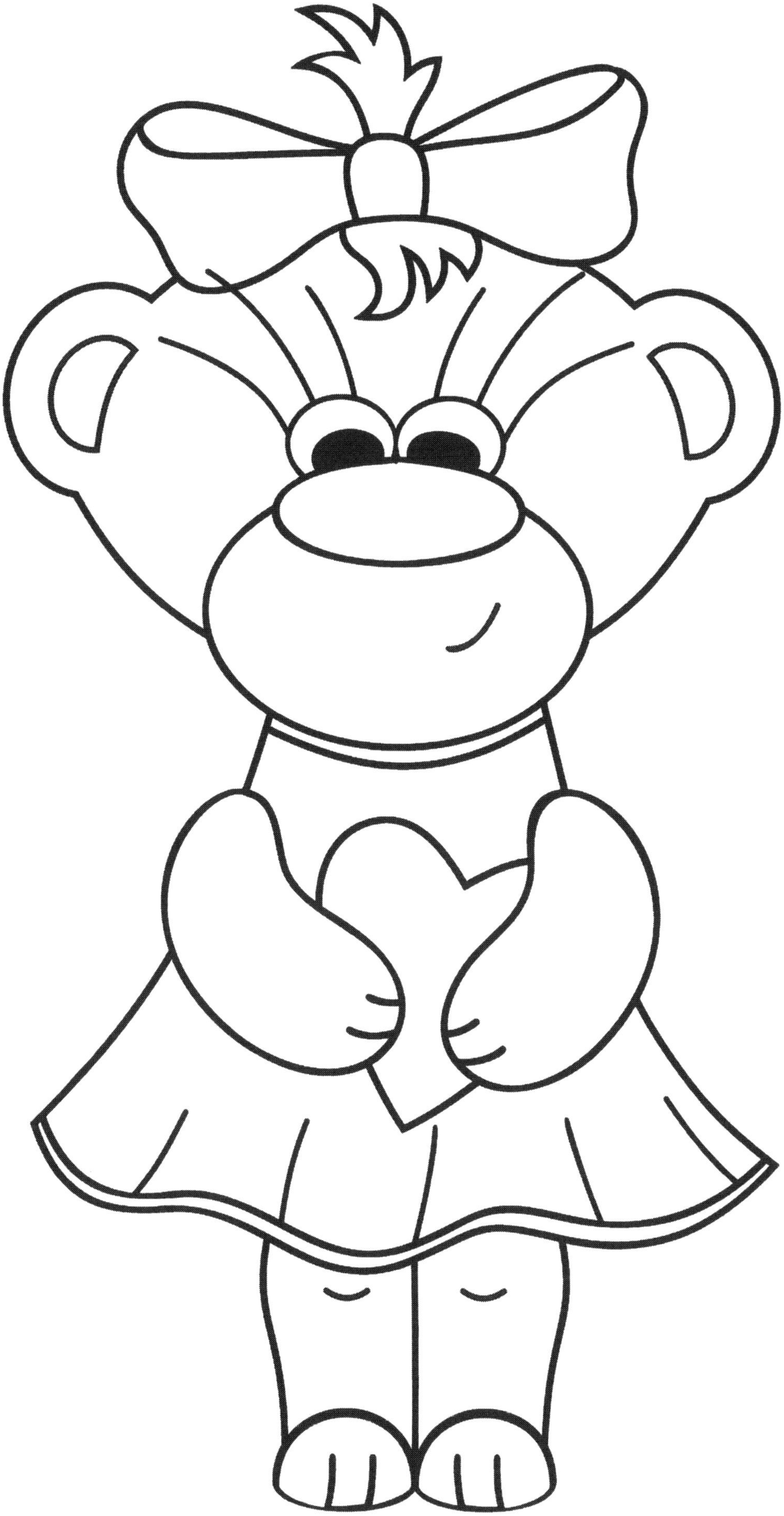

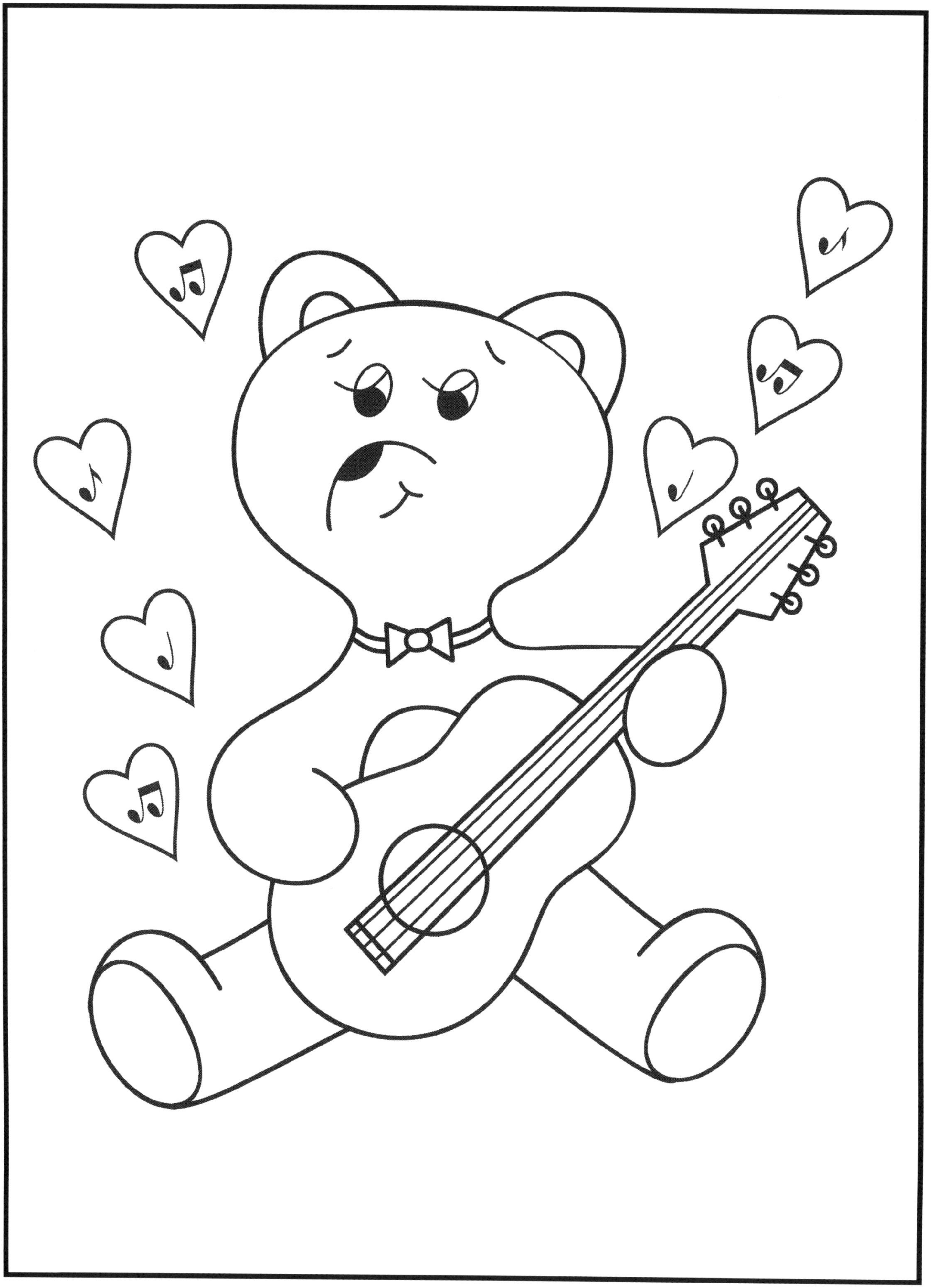

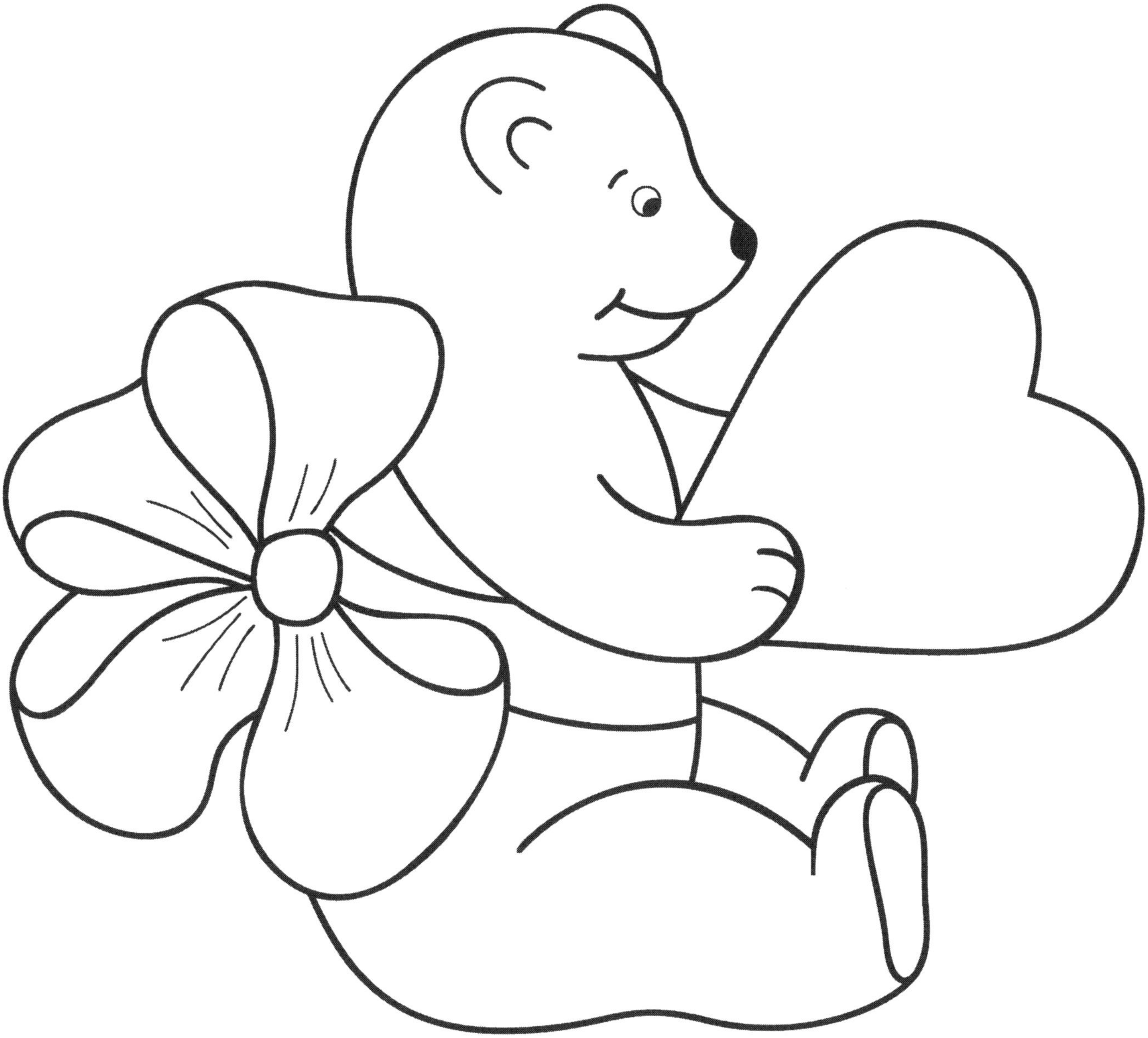

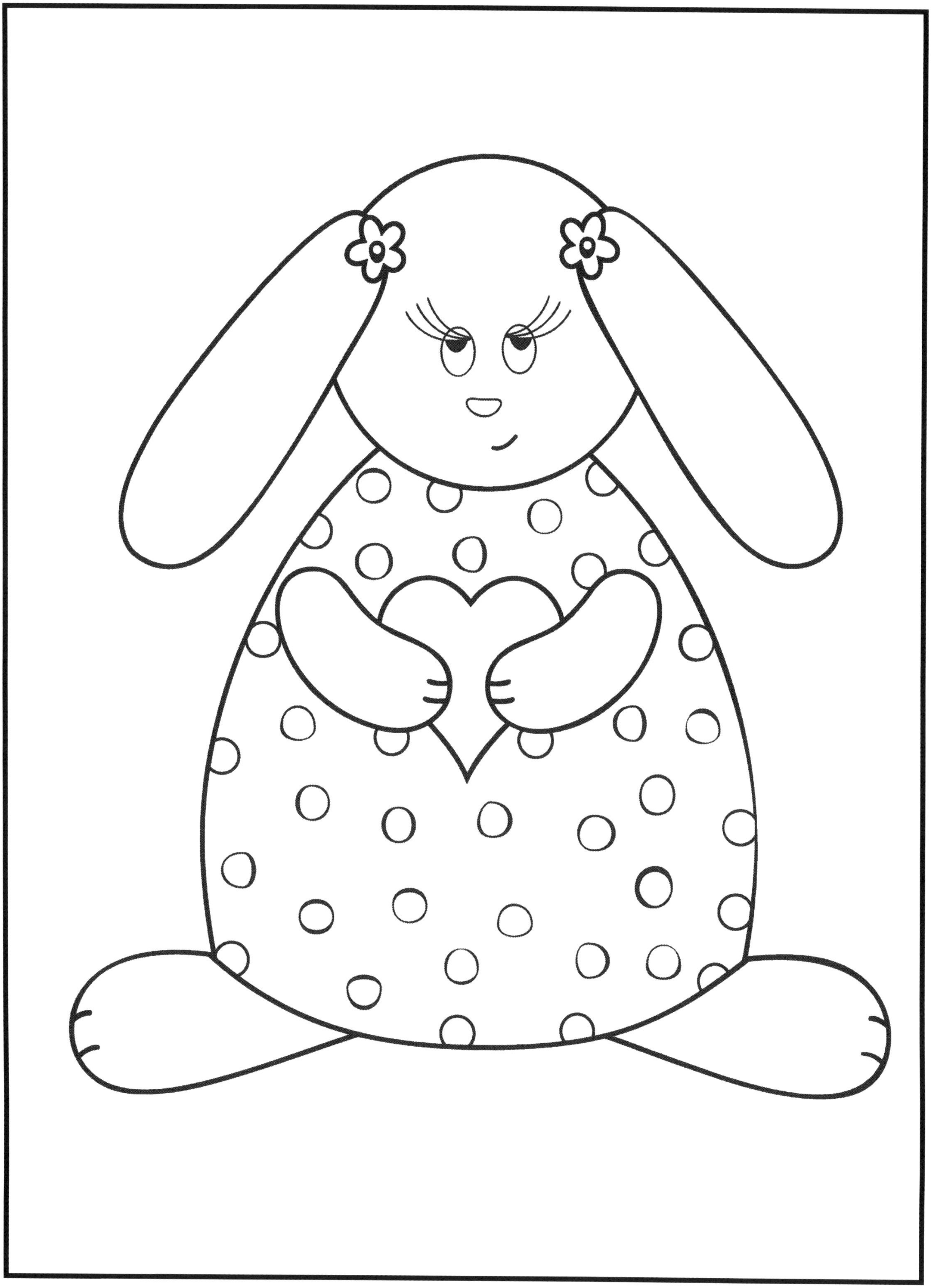

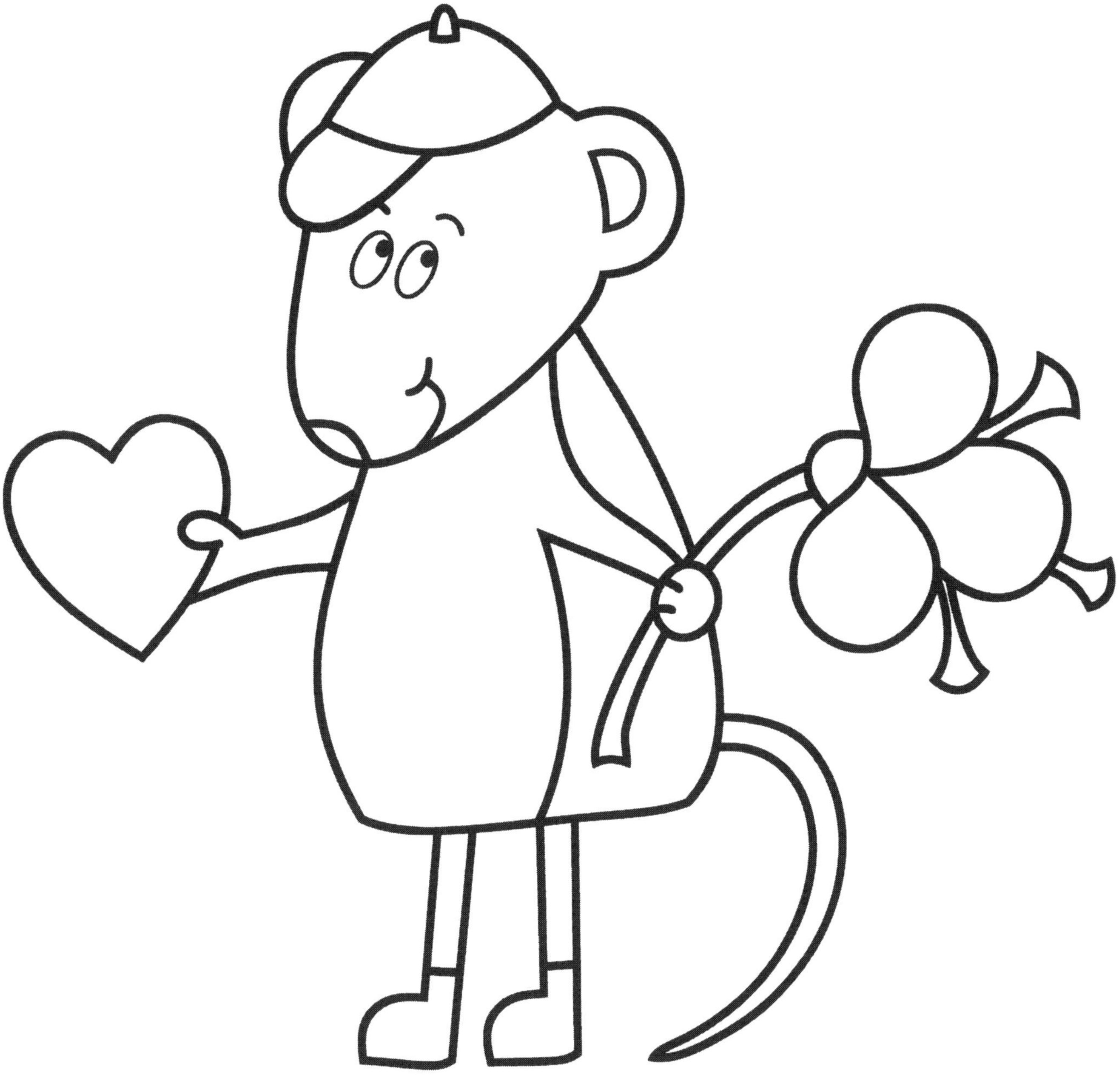

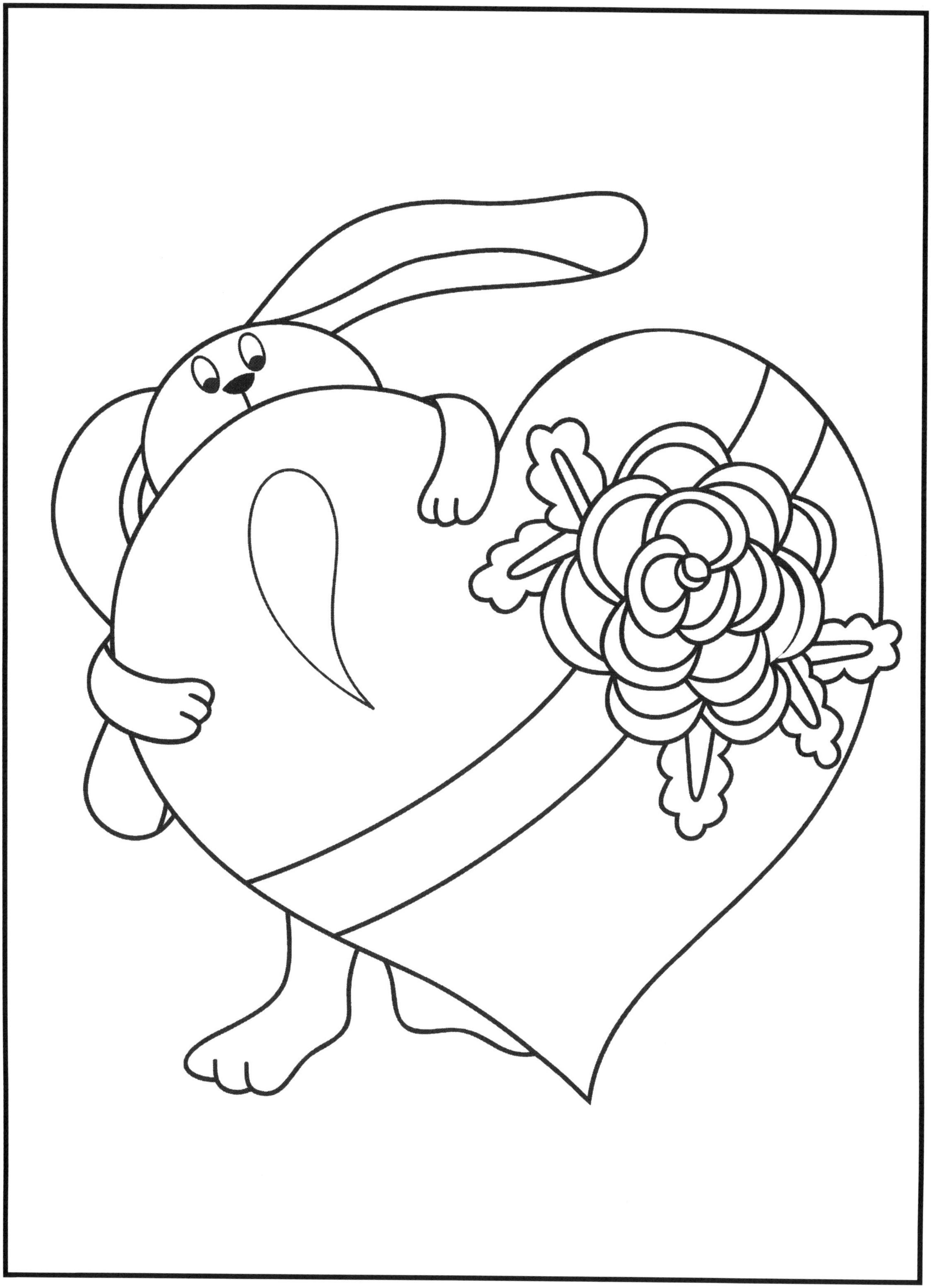

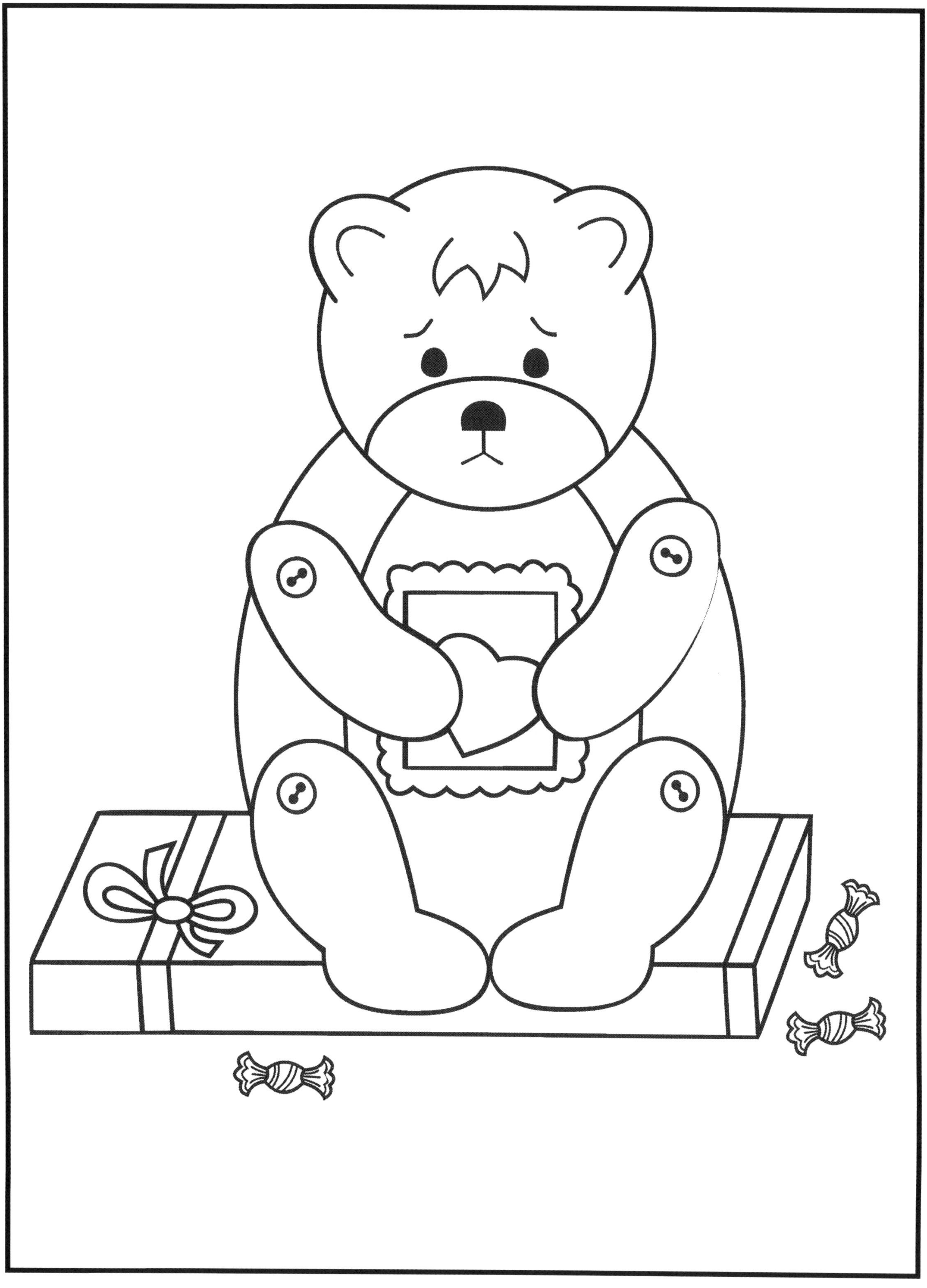

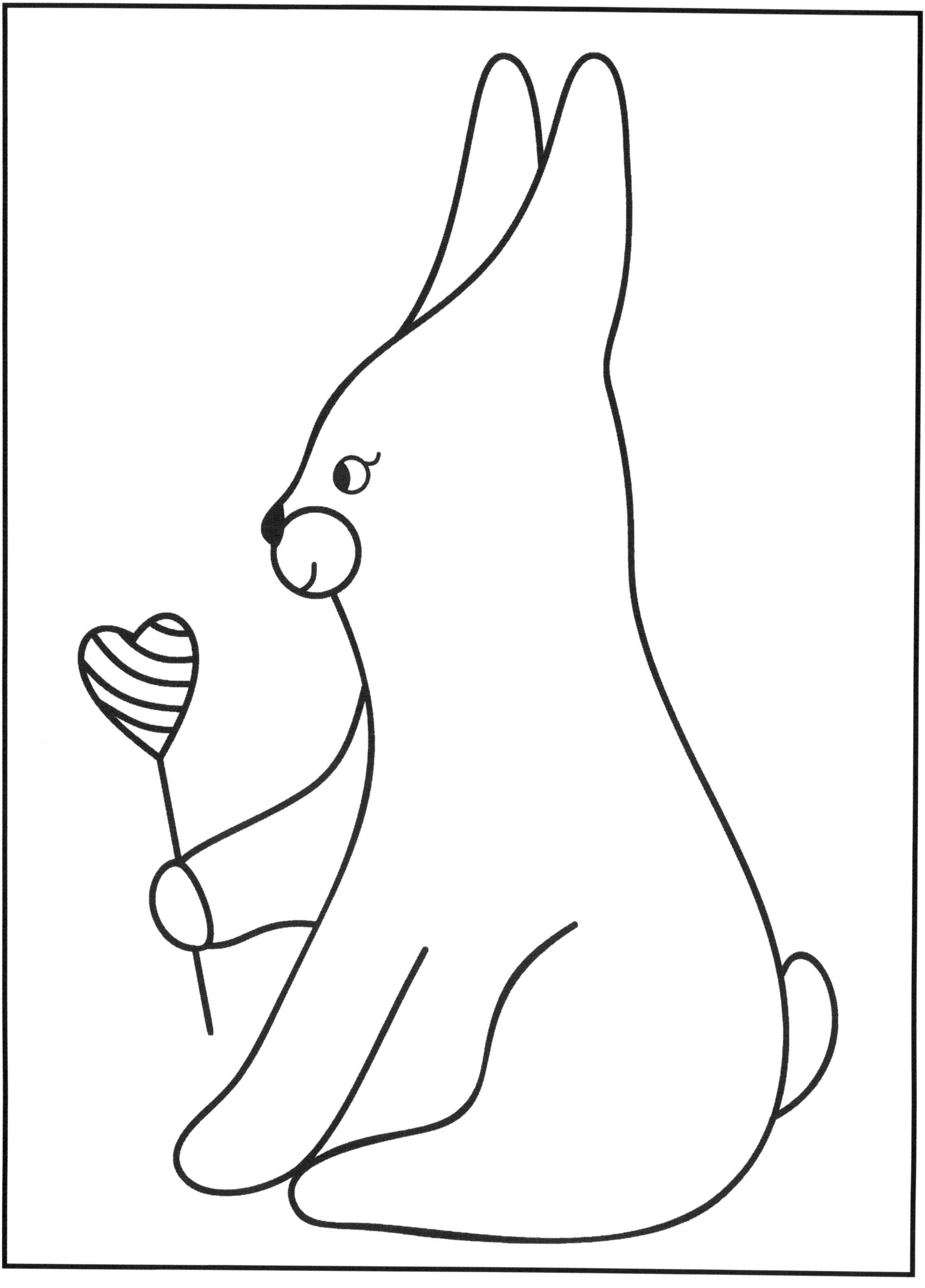

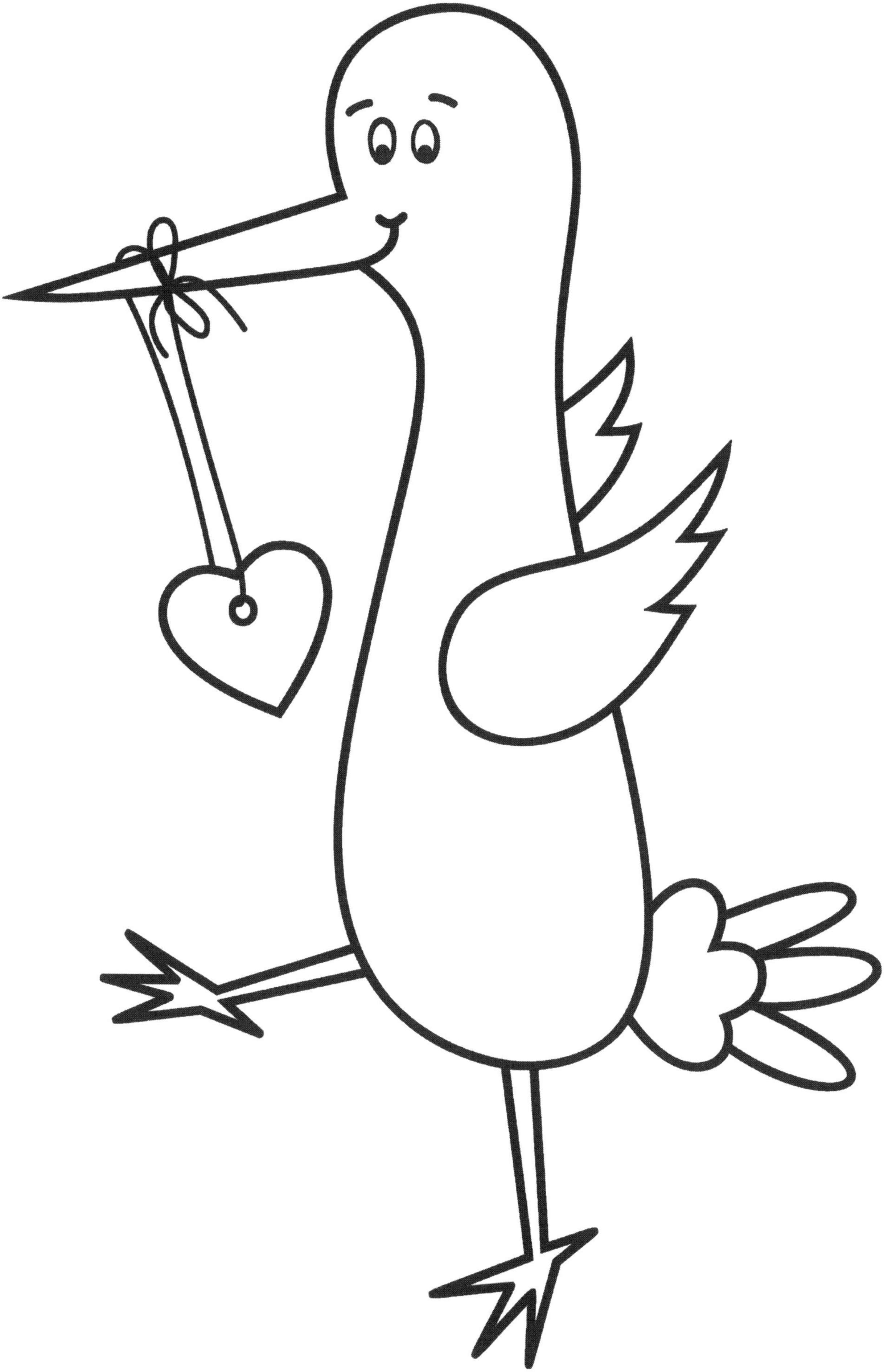

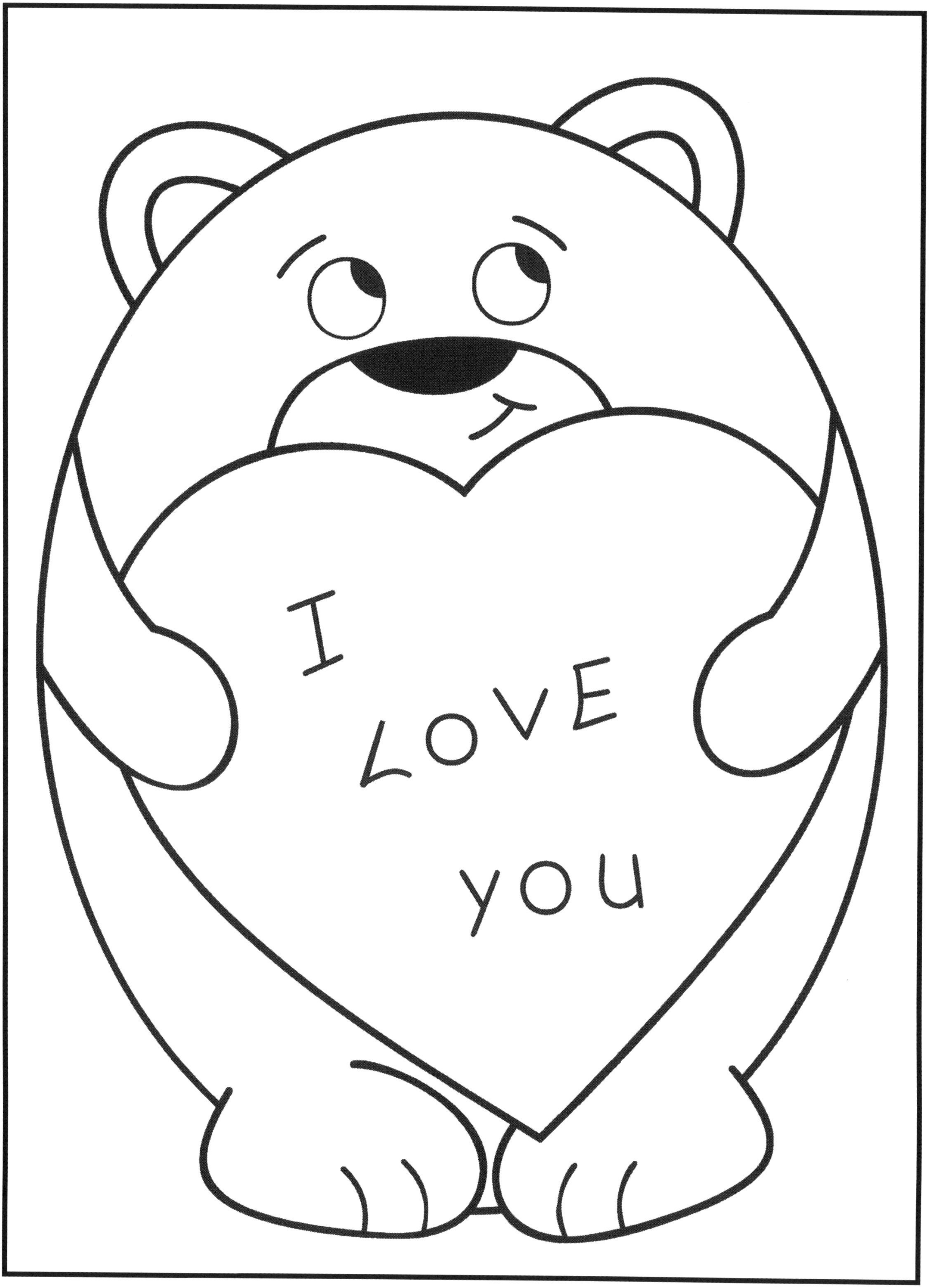
I
LOVE
you

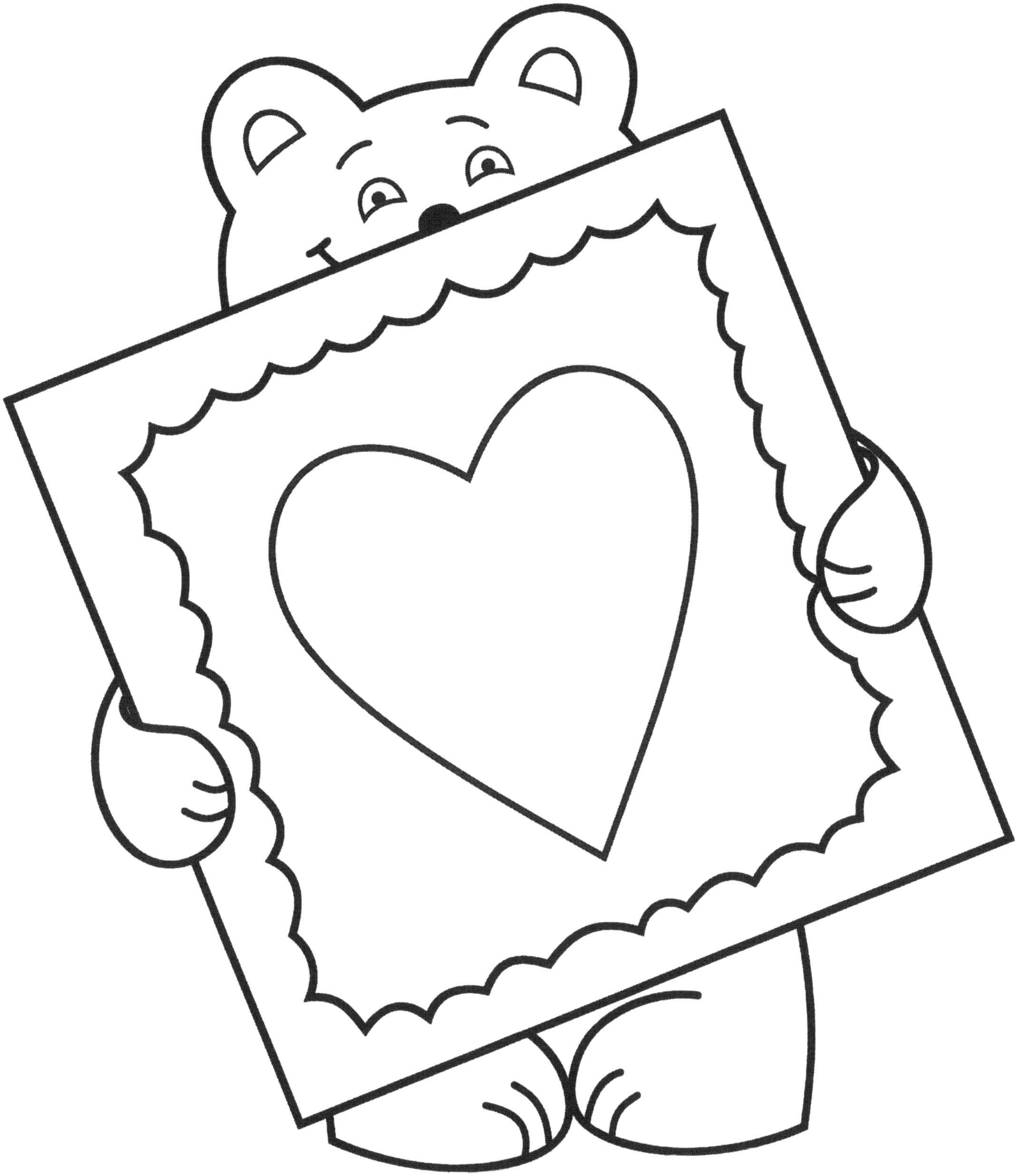

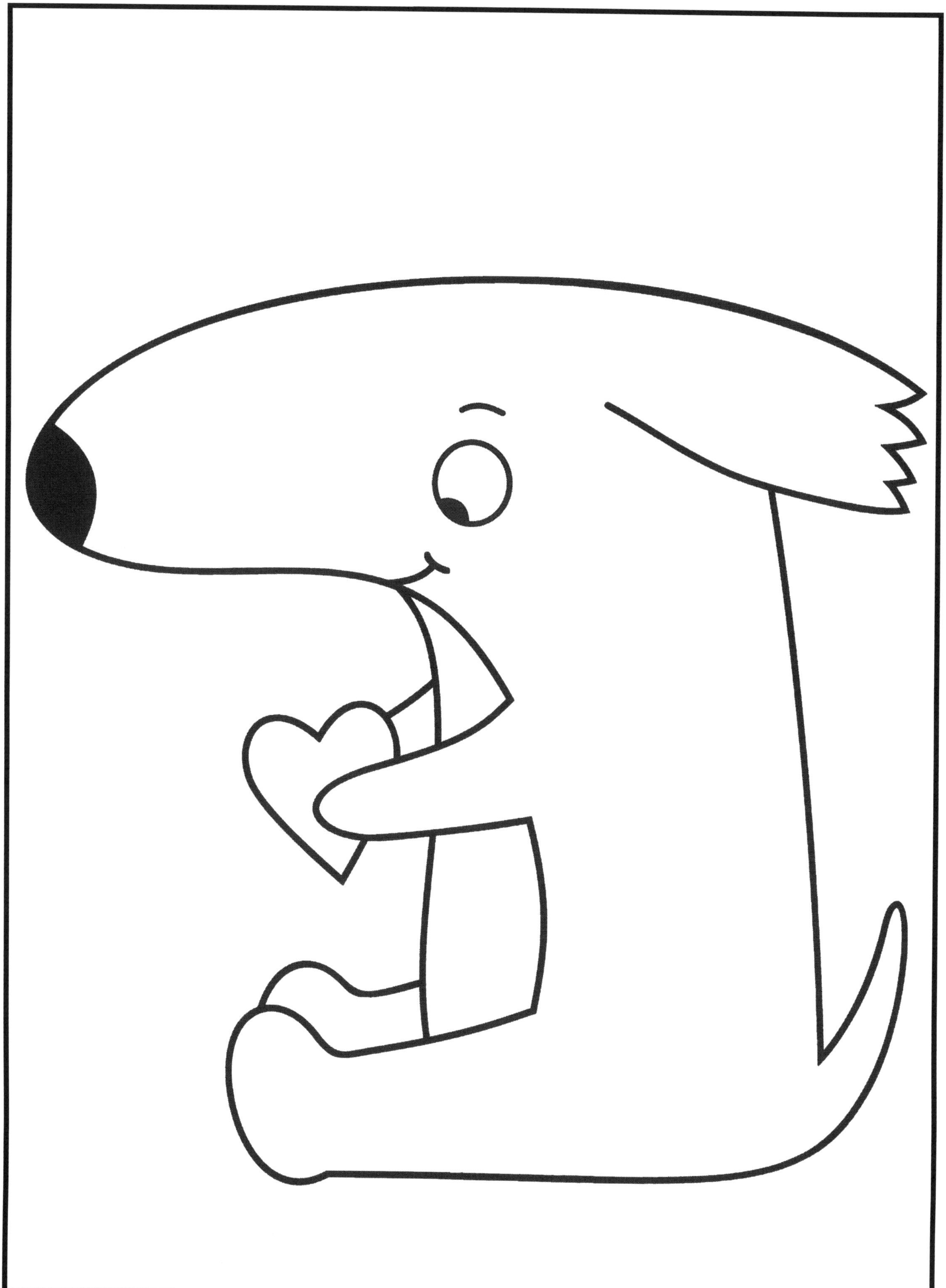

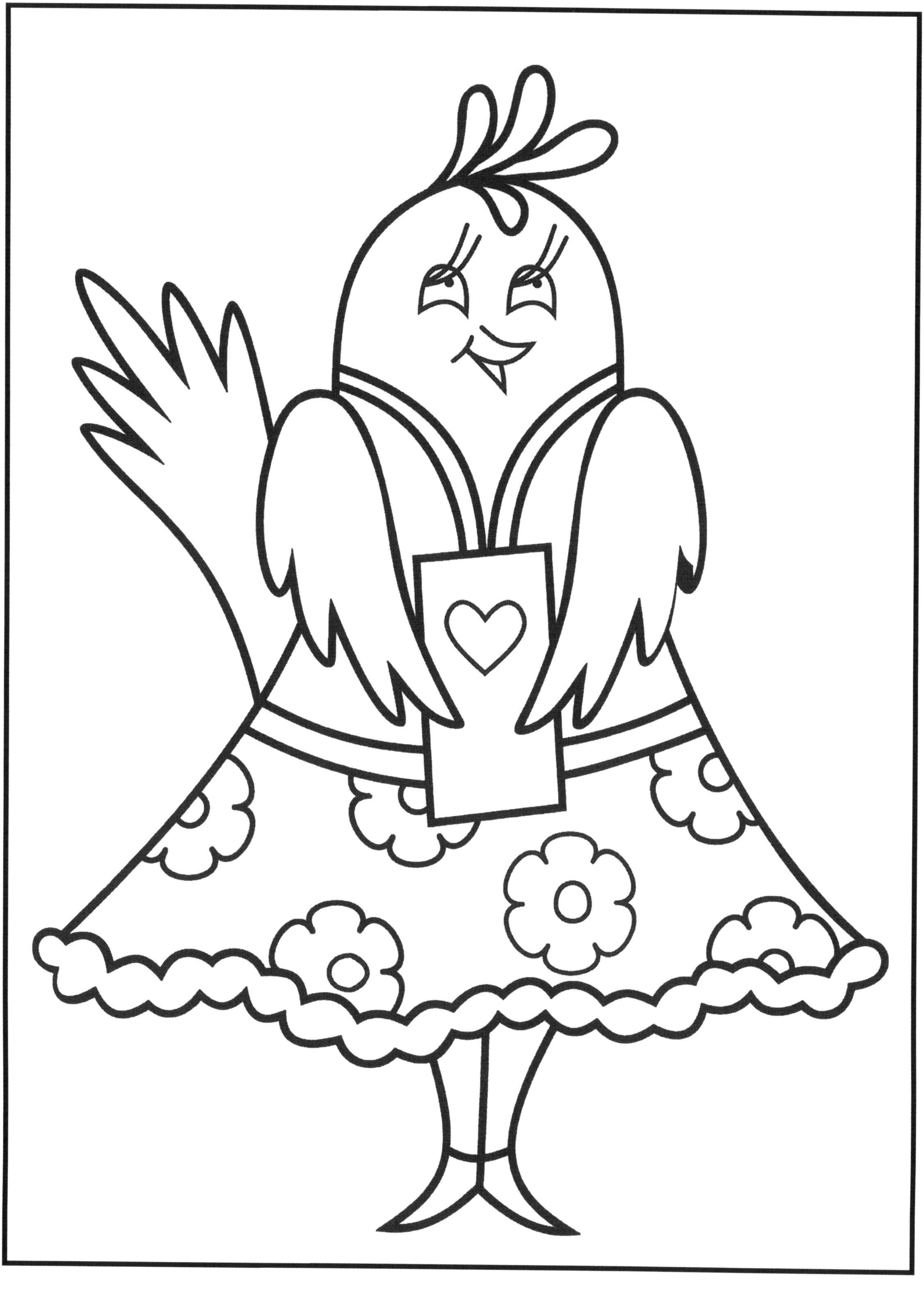

35099062R00046

Made in the USA
Middletown, DE
01 February 2019